STORIES FROM THE ISLANDS

BLASKET
Spirit

Anita Fennelly

Anita Fennelly

The Collins Press

First published in 2009 by
The Collins Press
West Link Park
Doughcloyne
Wilton
Cork

British Library Cataloguing in Publication Data
Fennelly, Anita
Blasket spirit
1. Fennelly, Anita 2. Spiritual retreats - Ireland - Great
Blasket Island 3. Great Blasket Island (Ireland) -
Description and travel
I. Title
914.1'96
ISBN-13: 9781905172900

Typesetting by The Collins Press
Typeset in Bembo 11 on 14 pt
Printed by CPI Cox and Wyman, UK

Photographs: pp. 47, 191 and back cover courtesy of Sigrid Gräser; p. 162
courtesy of Charles Haughey.

'. . . it is an ever-fixèd mark
That looks on tempests and is never shaken;
It is the star to every wandering bark . . .'

William Shakespeare, Sonnet 116.

This book is a gift to my wonderful daughter, Holly Heverin, and is dedicated to the memories of Frank Fennelly, my father; William Fennelly, my brother; Éanna Ó Broin, my friend.

Contents

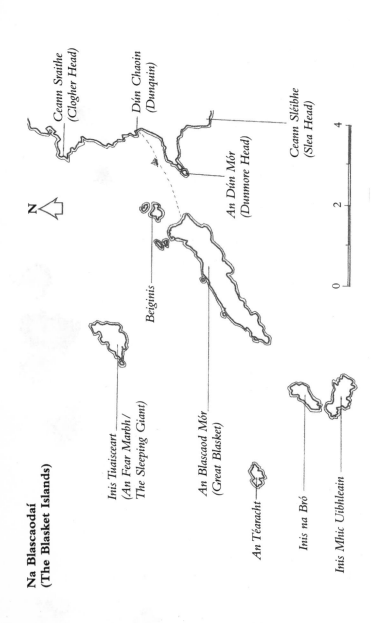

Na Blascaodaí
(The Blasket Islands)

Ceann Sraithe
(Clogher Head)

Dún Chaoin
(Dunquin)

Ceann Sléibhe
(Slea Head)

An Dún Mór
(Dunmore Head)

N

Beiginis

Inis Tuaisceart
(An Fear Marbh/
The Sleeping Giant)

An Blascaod Mór
(Great Blasket)

An Téaracht

Inis na Bró

Inis Mhic Uibhleáin

0   2   4

An Blascaod Mór
(The Great Blasket)

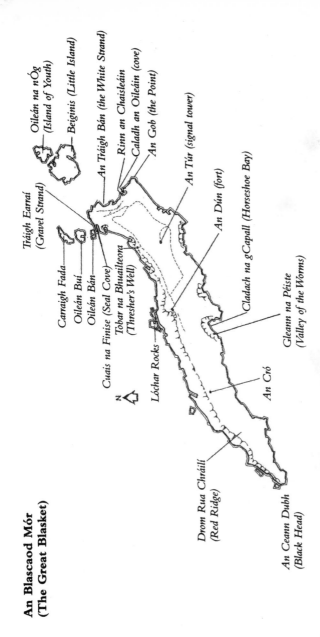

Oileán na nÓg (Island of Youth)

Beiginis (Little Island)

An Tráigh Bán (the White Strand)

Rinn an Chaisleáin

Caladh an Oileáin (cove)

An Gob (the Point)

An Túr (signal tower)

An Dún (fort)

Cladach na gCapall (Horseshoe Bay)

Gleann na Péiste (Valley of the Worms)

Tráigh Earraí (Gravel Strand)

Carraigh Fada

Oileán Buí

Oileán Bán

Cuais na Finise (Seal Cove)

Tobar na Bhuailteora (Thresher's Well)

Lóchar Rocks

An Cró

Drom Rua Chráilí (Red Ridge)

An Ceann Dubh (Black Head)

N

0   1

Acknowledgments

My grateful thanks are due to Ray and the late Joan Stagles, Sue Redican and all the island people for their hospitality, generosity and friendliness.

I owe sincere gratitude to the late Charles Haughey for his time, understanding, stories and the photograph of the red deer.

I am also most grateful to Maria Simonds-Gooding and to Larry Slattery for sharing their stories.

I am very grateful to Mai Fennelly, my mother, for her support and wonderful child-minding and to Seán Fogarty and Ray Heverin for their help with my trying computer skills.

Also many thanks to Ruth Byrne, Brian Coates, Kevin Collins, Paul Deavy, Jon Donovan, Maírín Jackson, Suzanne Kennedy, Pat Lee, Simon McAleese, Joe Malone, Karen Marsh, Patricia Murphy, Michael O'Meara, Karen O'Reilly, Des O'Sullivan, Kevin Power, Mary Shannon, Michael Shiel, Father Billy Swan, Karen Weekes, Ian Wright and my agent, Jonathan Williams.

First Days

In June, I settled into my tiny stone dwelling on the Great Blasket Island. The bad weather moved in with me. The clouds rolled in from the Atlantic, shrouding Slea Head, Dún Chaoin and the Three Sisters in a blanket of mist. Below the mist, white spray exploded on the dark cliffs of the Kerry coastline.

On the island, the ruined village was just visible under the cloud topping. The ferries stopped that day, leaving four Canadian tourists and me as the only overnight visitors. The Canadians disappeared over to the hostel, which used to be the home of the writer Peig Sayers in years gone by. I settled into my cowshed home, catching the leaks from the roof in a bucket and saucepan. My great plan to explore the island would have to be put on hold for a few days at least, the weather forecast being terrible. I resigned myself to reading and inventing endless menu variations of tinned fish and rice.

After two days and two nights, the relentless roar of the surf breaking on the White Strand was as familiar as my heartbeat. I insulated my cowshed by squashing wet moss and peaty soil into the holes where daylight gaped through the stone walls. I hung an old blanket over the door in a vain effort to keep the wind from whistling through the cracks. At times, the blanket billowed horizontally into the room, making nonsense of my endeavours. During the brief respites from the rainfall, I walked along the White Strand and wept. The roaring of the waves drowned my cries.

Three seals monitored my daily progress, ducking and bobbing in the rollers close to the shore. When I shouted, they came closer, eyeballing me curiously. They came so close, I could see their long white lashes and huge dark eyes. Looking into those eyes, I could believe that seals truly are the souls of drowned fishermen. At times, they lifted their heads and as one, turned their snouts away from the next wave. Occasionally, I could catch the sound of their barks over the waves. Early on, I christened them the Beverley Sisters.

Apart from the Beverley Sisters, my interaction with other living things was non-existent. Since I had waved goodbye to the ferryman and collected the key from the weaver, I had not spoken to another human being. I had noticed four colourful sets of Day-Glo rainwear bowed into the wind on the northern cliffs, beyond the strand. They had to belong to the Canadians. A man and woman moved frequently between the hostel and the cafe. Presumably they were the owners. I had not seen my ferryman since he disappeared into the white house on the southern end of the island the day the ferries stopped running. There seemed to be some other people in the white house too. From time to time, strains of fiddle music drifted on the wind over the island. An ache of loneliness cut through me every time I heard it. I wanted to go closer to the house to listen, but I never could. I could not handle the prospect of being invited in and having to make small talk. Back home, during the school term, I managed an Oscar-winning performance as teacher, comedienne and counsellor. After work, in the evenings, alone, I was consumed by the black comedy that had become my life. For several years I had felt as if I was observing my life from outside a window. I turned away from the ferryman's window and retreated into the sanctuary of my hut. It was easier that way.

From the one tiny window I could see the nearby island of Beiginis laced with a collar of billowing surf. Between it and the Great Blasket Island the red and blue ferries dipped and rocked helplessly. The Atlantic roared in the pit of my stomach. I sat on the sheepskin on the chair. Thirty minutes must have passed before I realised that I was staring again. My eyes had been fixed on the ferns and the pennywort plants growing from the walls around the bunk. For that half hour I had seen nothing, as my mind was dragged through the past few years yet again. Without my usual frantic distractions, the horror gripped me. Sickened with shock, I stood up and pulled on my saturated walking boots and raincoat. The rain drenched my face as I opened the door. I had to tire myself physically before I could sleep.

I headed up and around the south end of the island, the headland they call An Gob, leaving the ferryman's house far below. The fiddle was quiet. I imagined the two ferryman brothers having dinner with parents, wives and children. Once more, I could hardly see anything through the blur of tears. Salty water was what made the seals cry but I could blame the wind and driving rain. I leaned into the southwesterly wind and concentrated my mind on every laboured footstep as I climbed. The critical timing of breath and step obliterated the swirling grey world around me. Breath and step. In and out, on and up. Survival depended on clinging to the beat of breath and step. How long could I dull every cell in my body with the rhythm before a jolt of realisation, a lurch in my stomach winded me?

Suddenly I was forced to stop. A black-headed ewe blocked my path. She eyed me curiously, her soaked head cocked. I stared back at her helplessly. I wondered what she saw. Was I physically there at all? She did not move. The cloud had come right down on the cliff path before me. In the sea mist loomed the silhouettes of Inis Mhic Uibhleain and Inis na Bró. Darkness was falling quickly. The ewe held her ground.

She waited until I had stepped aside, defeated, before she trotted off the path into the mist and disappeared.

The cloud swirled around me, shrouding me in a cocoon of greyness. All definition and depth disappeared. One foot sank deep into a rabbit hole. The other foot struck an invisible rock, jolting my back. I had no sense of where I was. I stood silently as the sky floated by me. Through the veils of mist filtered the muffled thud of surf on the rocks far below. It became the one reality in my dark world. I stumbled in shadows. The rhythmic boom of the waves became the only thing to focus on. The sound was my salvation. I staggered blindly to the cliff edge.

Suddenly, the rhythm of the surf was broken, as voices pierced the cloud from close by. Giggles and chatter filled the air. As the mist drifted, I became aware of two small shadows above me on the path. They must have spotted me, for they were standing, facing my direction. I turned away from the cliff edge and struggled back up in the direction of the path, cutting in a safe distance ahead of the voices.

By the time I had rounded the headland, out of the mist and into the view of the deserted village, it was dark. The last of the grey light to the west of Inis Tuaisceart revealed the shapes of rocks, shoreline and the ruined village. As I came to the bottom of the path, and turned right past the well, I could see the yellow candlelit square of the weaver's door. I stopped and stared at the wonder of it for a while. Suddenly, the weaver's figure stood in the light and drew the darkness across it. I felt desperately alone.

As I fumbled with the bolt, I heard giggling behind me. The pair from the path had caught up on me. I couldn't open the door fast enough. I would have to turn and acknowledge them. In the rain and the darkness two figures came strolling down the path from the direction of the cafe. At the ruined cottage called the *Dáil*, just above my hut, they stopped. Were they looking at me? I couldn't tell if they could make out my form standing motionless in the dark shadow of the hut. On the other hand, I had the advantage of the western sky acting as their backdrop. They were young children. The taller of the two silhouettes had long skinny arms and matchstick legs under a knee-length dress. The smaller girl was the giddier one. They seemed to gaze in my direction for some time before the skinny one, squealing with delight, pulled her friend off down the hill. I heard one call the other 'Lish'. After they disappeared into the darkness, I went inside, lit a candle and put a pot of water on the gas stove. I felt shaken and strangely relieved.

The few words I had heard them speaking were in Irish. Maybe 'Lish' was short for 'Eilish'. The ferryman and his brother talked and joked in Irish. When they spoke on the VHF radio on the ferry, it was in Irish. Just like the young children on the pier in Dún Chaoin on the day I had crossed over to the island, these little girls spoke Irish effortlessly. When the little boy on the pier fell and cut his finger that day, wails and sobs punctuated his tragic account of the accident in Irish. When I tried to console him in English, he looked at me, confused, and ran off crying.

Next morning I was woken by a gentle scratching sound. I did not move, convinced that I had a mouse nosing around the shelf above my head. Only when I heard a chirp did I dare

View of the Dáil from inside Ray Stagle's cowshed.

to look. A cock robin had come in under the eaves, and was investigating my bag of Flahavan's porridge. Having satisfied himself with that, he fluttered down onto my walking boots and pecked busily at the wet clay on the toecap. Then, for no particular reason, he flew back up onto the shelf, ducked his head under the eaves and was gone.

It was 6 a.m. It had been my first uninterrupted night's sleep in over four years. I lay for some time in the warmth of the sleeping bag, aware of the unfamiliar feeling of rest and peace of mind. When I rose, I pulled on my raincoat and went out to the well to fill the saucepan. The air was cold and damp and the mist was still drenching. The living houses of the weaver and the ferryman and the hostel still slept. Their doors were closed. The dead houses of the village slumped against the hillside, their crumpled shells gaping stark and open. A rabbit nibbled furiously in the empty doorway of the old *Dáil* where the little girls had been the previous evening. I smiled now when I thought of them. I tried to convince myself that they could not have seen me at the cliff edge.

I read for most of that day and took the odd walk along the White Strand, accompanied as usual by the Beverley Sisters. Back in the hut I wore out a path between the chair and the door, keeping an eye out for the two little girls. Yet if I were to meet them again, I did not know if I would be able to bring myself to talk to them. I had my chocolate bar, the highlight of my rations, waiting for them on the shelf. By nine that night I had not seen them. The only people I had spotted all day were the four Canadians kicking a ball in the drizzle on the beach and the weaver emptying a basin of water out of the back of her cottage in the afternoon. It was dark now. I closed the door and wept. The radio usually distracted me, so I turned it on but, to my dismay, the exhausted batteries failed almost immediately.

It was then that I had my second encounter with the children. As I turned off the radio, I heard them giggling outside. I opened the door, casting a square of candlelight onto the two little girls who stood there, hand in hand. They both smiled and the smaller girl waved shyly at me. In the light I got a much clearer look at them. The smaller girl had thick black hair cut dead straight just below her ears, and an equally severe style of fringe. Her broad smile revealed a big gap in the front where her baby teeth had been. She must have been six or seven years old. First Holy Communion photographs are synonymous with toothless smiles. 'Hello', I said. They just giggled. I tried my best '*Dia dhuit*'. That elicited no response either. I should have said '*Dia dhaoibh*'. Perhaps my feeble attempt at Irish was nothing they could understand. We continued to smile at each other. The little girl stood with her feet turned in, each set of toes taking turns to cover the other. The weaver always walked around barefoot too: it seemed the most practical thing to do on the island, but not the warmest on such a wet night. I asked the children if they would like some chocolate. True to form, they continued to prattle in Irish, and ignored what I'd said. In anticipation of the robin's dawn visit, I had put the chocolate in my robin- and mouse-proof jar. When I came back to the door, the children had gone; I just glimpsed them disappearing into the ruins below my path. By the time I had my coat on, and had found the torch, there was no sign of them. I wondered at their parents allowing them to wander around in the dark. Then I wondered at my own judgmental attitude. This was surely the way to bring up children: laughing and carefree. Two grubby faces with two equally grubby dresses, playing with rabbits, donkeys and lambs, in sand, sea and heather.

I ended up below the ferryman's house. Inside, the fiddle started up and shadows passed across the butter-yellow of the candlelit squares. I guessed the girls were running between the cafe and the ferryman's house. I considered knocking on the door and leaving in the chocolate for them, but lost the courage before I had barely formed the idea.

When the robin woke me on his dawn expedition the next morning, I realised that, once again, I had had a full night's sleep. I turned over and watched him pecking at the crumbs I had left on the floor beside my boots, which stood dark, heavy, cold and sodden with water. I decided that I would not bother with them that day. (In fact, I never bothered with them again for the rest of my stay on the island.)

The thrill of walking on wet grass, peat, heather, sand and sea in bare feet never diminished. My feet felt alive. I felt alive! I walked around the northwest of the island in the rain. My feet slid into puddles of brown peaty water, then gripped on dead heather roots at the path's edge. I reached the place known as the crossroads, the belt buckle of the island where the north and south roads join. From here, the paths merged and disappeared up along the spine of the island and into the mist. I opted to return on the southern path that I had walked the previous evening in the dark. One false step and I would tumble almost 300 metres to my death. It would be like falling off a roof, the steepest and highest roof in the world. I shuddered when I realised how close I had been to that fall.

Later, back in the hut, I was absorbed and busy. I swept out the sand and the grass with a bunch of dead heather branches that I had tied together with a hair band. I washed out some clothes in a basin by the well. I searched the beach for hollow stones, which would act as safe holders for my candles and tea lights. Finally, I made a little pot of vegetable stew, adding wild thyme and nettle leaves picked on my walk. In the glow of my new candlelight arrangement, I sat down to enjoy my dinner.

Just then, I heard the two little girls approach the door. I was ready with the chocolate this time as I opened the door. They stood there, hand in hand yet again, beaming at me. Before I could say a thing, they waved at me and took off down the hill and into the ruin.

I called out and followed them. There was no sign of them in the ruin, but I knew they were watching me. 'Well, if you don't want your chocolate, I'll just have to leave it for the rabbits.' With that, I held up the chocolate bar and pretended to place it on the crumbling windowsill. 'Enjoy it, rabbits. *Slán.*' I sauntered back to the hut, watching out of the corner of my eye. I couldn't spot them but I knew they had me under observation. I giggled to myself back inside. How long would it be before they ran past again, looking for their chocolate on their way home? By the time an hour had passed, I had heard nothing, so I sneaked down to the ruin. There was no sign of them.

Next morning, the robin woke me and the sound of thundering waves surged through me. I lay there feeling quite pleased with myself. I thought of the two funny little girls, and laughed aloud. The bird stopped pecking and looked up, startled by the unexpected sound. We looked at each other momentarily; then he resumed his breakfast. I quietly opened my book, *The Blasket Islands* by Joan and Ray Stagles, and picked up reading from where I had left off the previous night. A seagull feather marked the chapter on the village and its houses; a small map on the next page showed each dwelling-house on the island, and gave its owner's name. I searched for the little cowshed in which I was sleeping. It was Joan and Ray Stagles who had put the roof on the cowshed, which was clearly marked on the map below the well called Tobar na Croise. With the seagull feather I traced down to house number 3, the building that my two little friends always played in. It was marked as the old National School. I fell asleep again.

I woke some time later to the sound of water sloshing outside at the well, where my ferryman stood, toothbrush in hand and a blue towel draped around his shoulders. 'I'm taking the Canadians off the island this morning. There's another huge depression coming in, and the long-range forecast is bad, so if you want to get off the island, you'd better be ready at the slipway in ten minutes.'

I was stunned. The urgency of what he was suggesting was out of sync with my pace of life over the previous few days. Realising he needed to clarify himself, he added, 'Seán is closing the cafe and going out to the mainland too. We'll be taking the ferries into shelter in Dingle, so you'll have no way off unless you come now.'

I didn't know what to do. Why would I go back to the mainland? 'When will you be coming back to the island again?' I asked.

'Isn't that what I'm telling you? I don't know. The long-range forecast isn't good. It will only be yourself and the weaver on the island if you stay.'

'So you're all going off. You're taking your family off too?'

'Lorcan's taking his own boat across.'

From his look, I knew he was losing patience. 'And the children – you'll be taking them across too?'

'I don't have children.' He looked at me impatiently. 'Now are you coming or what?'

'Sorry. They must belong to someone in the hostel then.'

'There are no children in on the island. There's Seán in the cafe and Laura, four Canadian walkers, me, my brother and three other fellas, the weaver and yourself. Now, are you coming?'

All I wanted to do was run inside. The heat of confusion burned through me. There *were* children on the island. I had met them *three* times. I could not understand why he would deny their existence.

He started off down the path, calling 'You've got ten minutes. The weather won't wait.' I went back into the hut and sat on the chair. I could not get motivated to roll up my sleeping bag and pack my stove and the few things. After ten minutes, it was evident that some part of me had made a decision. I was going to remain in on the Great Blasket Island.

I walked down the path to the cliff overlooking the slipway. The two brothers were lowering the inflatable dinghy into the water. The dark-haired man and the woman from the hostel climbed aboard with their bags and a little pup. Two other young men followed, carrying an empty gas cylinder. The ferryman shouted at the third man, who had remained on the slipway to help people aboard. The sea was choppy, spray soaking the passengers and their bags as the dinghy struggled out to meet the red ferry, which swayed up and down like a demented rocking horse. As I watched, the four Canadians hurried down the path behind me, straining under the weight of enormous backpacks. 'Hello there. We didn't see much of you for the past few days!'

I just smiled. 'No' was all I could think of saying. The first man lingered, seeing that they were on time for the ferry after all.

'Are you staying out on the island?' Strange the way he said 'out on the island.' The locals and the old islanders always said 'in on the island.' The island was the heart, the centre, the 'in'.

'Yes, I'm staying in on the island.'

'Gee, you could be in for some pretty rough weather!'

'Not too bad I hope. Is everybody else leaving the hostel too?'

'Yep, Seán and Laura have gotten down there before us. It's all shut up now.'

Only Seán and Laura, who managed the cafe, had gone down before them with the ferrymen and the three other men. There were no children to be seen. I stood on the cliff and watched the two ferries disappear across the Blasket Sound and around the headland into Dingle Bay.

I was baffled. The only people with whom I had had any contact over the past few days were the two children, and yet nobody in the hostel or in the ferryman's house knew anything about them. As I came back up from the landing slip, I could see smoke rising from the weaver's chimney: she would regard my visit as odd, after my apparent unfriendliness over the previous five days.

The yellow door was open as usual. I called out, unable to see anything in the darkness inside. Her voice answered. 'Hello. So you've not left then? Come in.'

I stepped inside the room. I couldn't see a thing. Outside, the brightness of the sky dropped into the sea on all sides. Inside, two tiny windows, cluttered high with books and baskets of wool, ensured that the small room remained almost totally dark. As my eyes adjusted, I met her smile. 'Clear a space and sit down,' she said. She stood at the table, elbow-deep in a bowl of flour. I didn't know where to start. Stacks of woven rugs, shawls and baskets were everywhere. Balls of different coloured yarn littered the floor, like dozens of young feeding off the great wooden loom in the centre. I stepped onto the hearth, the only free space available. 'Just put the rugs on top of that lot and you'll find a chair,' she said helpfully. I moved as much stuff as I could, and then perched myself on the edge of an ancient-looking chair. 'So are you enjoying your stay in Ray's?'

'Yes, it's got everything I need, thank you.'

'You won't be able to walk too far for the next few days. The weather's set to turn bad. Fergal and Lorcan will be sheltering the ferries in Dingle, so you're in for a quiet time here.'

'Yes, one of them told me.'

She began to knead the dough on the table. After a while she asked, 'Did you get to walk to the back of the island yet?'

'No. I've only been over the hill to where the two cliff roads meet. The mist was too bad to go any farther. Is it far to the end?'

'Three miles. From the crossroads, you continue on up the next hill to the Iron Age fort. From there, the path is close to the cliff, and it's a 300-metre sheer drop to the right. The island falls at the western end to a site with the remains of beehive huts and then there's nothing but sea. I don't get to walk to the back of the island much in the summer, except when there's no ferry running. Then I can catch up on some weaving and close the door when I want to and go walking.'

She continued flouring a tray and cutting a cross in the top of the bread without once throwing a glance in my direction. Her ease and detachment made me relax. She was well used to hundreds of curious tourists passing through her one-room island shop. I was just one more. I watched her fill the bowl with hot water from the kettle and wash up the baking things. I offered to dry and she handed me a teacloth.

'Now we can have a cup of tea,' she smiled. As I relished my scone and jam, she told me that her name was Sue, that she was Welsh, and that she had been living on the Great Blasket Island for seventeen years. She made her living weaving and selling her work to summer visitors on the island. During the very bad winter weather she stayed out on the mainland.

By the time I had finished my second cup of tea, I still had not mentioned the children. Part of me was beginning to wonder if I had finally lost my mind. I rose to leave, aware that she had to make the most of the daylight to do her weaving. 'Were there any children staying on the island over the past few days?' I suddenly heard myself blurt out, as I stopped in the doorway.

'No, we haven't had children up in the hostel since a German family stayed there over a month ago.'

I explored every ruin in the Blasket village that day. There wasn't sight nor light of anybody. I went across to the hostel. Both half-doors were padlocked. Beyond it, the cafe, too, was shut and deserted. As the rain got heavier and the wind picked up, I retreated to my little home and settled down, determined to read. I couldn't concentrate. I kept thinking of the children and, strangely, I became more and more convinced that they knew everything about me. After dinner, it got dark quickly. Sue would have finished her weaving. I pulled on my raingear and headed down to her glowing doorway. A fire burned in the hearth and the two chairs were pulled up in front of it.

We talked until I could hardly make out her face in the glow of the dying fire. It was time for her to light a candle and head to bed, ready for first light and another day of weaving. As she closed the door on the night air, I set off up the steep path towards my little home. I felt light and relaxed after the warmth of the fire and our friendly chat.

Above the hillside rose a half-moon, glossing the edges of billowing clouds. Below, surf roared on the strand. Across the Blasket Sound the great dark bulk of the mainland slept. A distant beam of headlights pierced the night sky as a car crossed over the mountain road from Dingle and disappeared. Over there was another world.

I turned back to my world and my climb back up the hill. This time I had no warning of chatter or laughter: the two children stood hand in hand in front of me. Their stare bored through my chest, vibrating through my whole body.

They knew every aspect of my life and yet they smiled at me silently. I said nothing either and smiled at them. I don't know how long we stood there, looking at each other. I was conscious of the rain beginning to fall and trickle down my face. They remained perfectly dry. I should have noticed that before when I saw them running around in the rain. As they gazed at me, I felt a wave of sadness come over me. On some level I was aware that I would not see them again. I did not dare divert my gaze.

As they began to fade before my eyes, I could see the smaller girl dancing from foot to foot as she had done the last time I had seen her. The skinny girl was waving to me as they disappeared. Suddenly, I could feel the coldness of the rain, the wind and the surf roaring in my ears. There was nothing but dark, wet grass on the pathway before me. I knew I would not see them again. There was no more need.

The following morning, as I set off on my first trek to the back of the island, I called in on Sue. She declared an official tea break and we sat on an old bench outside her door watching two choughs teaching their chicks how to fly. Once again I had slept the whole night through and felt as confident and relaxed as I had done during the previous evening's chat. As I passed by the ruins of the old National School, I took the chocolate bar that I had been saving for the little girls and placed it inside on the hearth. Perhaps it was only the wind and the sea that heard my thanks.

I never saw the two little girls after that night on the Great Blasket Island and I never spoke about them until the night the three sheep farmers stayed in on the island.

Páidí's Trail

The gale blew from the north for several days. Towards the end of the week I was woken constantly during the night by violent gusts funnelling through the gaps in the walls. Manx shearwater flew in from the sea over the island. In the darkness their chilling human-like cry sent shivers up my spine. It is said of the shearwater's cry that it led to tales of wailing banshees in our ancestors' time. I burrowed deeper into my sleeping bag.

I slept late. When I woke, I could hear nothing but gusting wind and the roar of the surf below. White horses fled before violent gusts along the Blasket Sound. The forecasts had predicted winds from the north increasing to storm force. There would be no ferries appearing for several more days.

Despite the cold wind, the island was bathed in sunshine. A dolphin nuzzled the barrel moorings below and jumped friskily between the buoys. We would have the island to ourselves again. I took my towel and set off through the ruins down to the cliff path and then headed towards the beach. I inched my way down the slippery cliff to the White Strand. The sand was dark and cold after days of rain. I abandoned my clothes on a flat rock in the shelter of a cove at the village end and raced into the waves. Initially, the assault of the breakers numbed any feeling of cold. I whooped and gasped as I ducked and slapped my hands over my body in an attempt at a cursory wash. The dolphin continued to play, favouring the black barrels over the manic white spectacle thrashing around in the shallows. Within seconds, I was back on the beach, wrapped in my towel, chattering and stamping my feet.

After a late breakfast of porridge, honey and black tea, I set off on my daily expedition. I chose the south path, away from the wind. Once I had climbed high and had turned the corner of An Gob, I left behind the deafening noise of the wind and the waves.

The shelter and stillness were staggering. Skylarks hovered in blue light and sang their hearts out. Suddenly, they plummeted like stones into the heather and disappeared before their song took flight again.

Wheatears obligingly alighted on rocks or bracken against the skyline, as if ready for inspection. They looked smart, in fashionable silver with black wings and matching black eyeliner. I began to recognise their habits. The wheatear ducks its head, neck and chest forwards and back, like a rocking horse, as it chirps cheerfully. The crested skylark sinks its head right down into its shoulders as it sings. Pipits and wheatears stitched a haphazard path for me, making my progress slow.

I had only just made it around the first turn when I met Sue wending her way home. She was wearing a thin rain jacket and was soaked to the skin. She was tanned peanut-brown and barefoot. 'Have you seen the choughs?' she called. I hadn't. I had been absorbed by the wheatears, following their trail like Hansel and Gretel's crumbs. 'Have a look. The young have learned so fast.' She took the big binoculars from around her neck and offered them to me. I could see the choughs with their scarlet red bills skirting the cliffs over 30 metres below. Their deep-throated caw carried on the wind.

'Did you see Donie playing again this morning? Your door was still closed when I left for the back of the island, so I didn't like to wake you up.'

'You mean the dolphin? I didn't know he had a name.'

'Yes, he's called after Donie the ferryman.'

I remembered Donie, his sunburned skin red between his freckles, sitting in the dinghy in blazing sunshine the previous summer. I had offered him my sunscreen: I had never seen sunburn like it. 'I wouldn't be using that stuff,' he laughed. I left the sunscreen behind on the boat, pretending that I had forgotten to take it with me.

'He was still playing with the barrels when I set off this morning.' Sue spotted another bird and directed my gaze along lines of heather and over rocks to where a little bird was perching on a tuft of heather. I would never have spotted him. He was a stonechat and his proud little rosy breast and gleaming white neck scarf hanging down over his shoulders made him look both distinguished and distinguishable from a distance. Then, as if he knew he had acquired two admirers, he flew back to a tuft of heather on the skyline, giving himself the ideal backdrop with which to highlight his magnificent plumage.

'What the mind does not know the eye does not see.' The saying was so true. Once Sue had opened my mind to wheatears and choughs, my eyes began to see them everywhere. I had never seen the stonechats before, although they had been all around me. Now I would see them for the rest of that day and every day.

'Donie is much younger than Fungie, the Dingle dolphin, and he has a lot more energy. He began following the ferry from Dún Chaoin and then gradually began to stay around the island. Lately, he appears just after dawn below Páidí Dunleavy's. He frolics around in the surf there for hours.'

Talk turned to Páidí Dunleavy. Páidí was the only one of the original islanders who maintained the roof on his house and who returned faithfully every summer to live in the old ways. His cottage stood out like a beacon, even from the mainland. Unlike the tumbling grey ruins of the village, Páidí's home was whitewashed. It was roofed in black felt and had its windows and door painted chocolate brown. It stood on the cliff edge above the beach. Right in front of it, Sue pointed out Rinn an Chaisleáin.

Rinn an Chaisleáin was a small, bare headland covered with a scattering of lichen-speckled rocks. I *had* noticed them. Each one stood oddly from the grass like a jagged tooth. She explained that these strange little stones marked the unconsecrated graves of infants, shipwrecked sailors and suicides who were not taken to the mainland for a church burial. After hearing that, I could never pass without leaving some wild flowers among the stones. Back in from this strange graveyard was Páidí Dunleavy's cottage.

By all accounts, Páidí was a character. He liked his drop of whiskey, his music and a good *seisiún*. Sue laughed as she recalled the story of his being wheeled home one night in a wheelbarrow. Unlike other islanders on the mainland, Páidí had no time for chatting to journalists and giving interviews. He scoffed at 'the romanticising that they go on with. Life is tough but you get on with it.' He was also infuriated by a report claiming that what had finally caused the islanders to evacuate the island was their confinement during three stormy weeks without being able to open the door even once. He nearly blew a gasket. 'What do they think we did? Piss out the window?' Many an ego-punctured journalist was seen retreating down the path to the pier, tail between his legs, Páidí's wrath ringing in his ears.

Sue spoke with great fondness for the old man as we stood surveying the village. To fishermen, sheep farmers and summer tourists, Sue had become the island matriarch. Many a storm she had weathered over the seventeen years, spinning and weaving on the island alone. The VHF radio operated from her house. For seafarers, she was the voice on the Blasket. To the steady stream of exhausted tourists and strays that flopped onto her doorstep in the summer months she offered drink, rest and a friendly ear. Páidí had certainly taken to this vivacious Welsh woman. In latter years he walked her around to the lovers' bench. Courting couples used to meet there, safe from the censure of village eyes. He showed her the names of friends long departed either to the New World or the Next World, which were etched into the rock. Today, the rough stone seat is only surveyed by kittiwakes and the odd black-backed gull that drifts by. The only ones to linger and play there are the nibbling rabbits.

'Páidí was determined to leave his mark. Every summer when he was in on the island he would find another wall or a rock to carve his name on. Have you seen it?'

'No, and I've been in every ruin on the island.'

'Well, it's like you say: "What the mind doesn't know, the eye doesn't see." You'll begin to see his name all over the place now. One of his most conspicuous signatures is on the plaster on the gable wall of the Kearney house, just below the schoolhouse.'

I had wandered through there many times and had never noticed anything of the sort. But then, I was otherwise distracted.

'Another place that Páidí used to visit, when he was in, was a huge slab of rock in Gleann na Péiste. Half the islanders who ever lived here carved their names into it. Every summer, if he was strong enough, he would make the same pilgrimage back to the glen to carve his name and the year. Every year he told me it would be his last, and soon there would be nothing left of him but his name. Then, one year, it came true.' With that, Sue slung her binoculars around her neck again. 'I must get back and dry out. I'm going down on the low tide to pick lichen off the rocks.'

'What colour do you get from that?'

'A rich golden tan. It depends on the time of year you pick the lichen though. The shades can vary a lot.'

'If you need a hand, I'll come down when I get back.'

'Great, but don't cut your walk short.'

'Well, I won't go to the end. The wind is lethal, so I might just climb up to the fort. Do I pass anywhere near Gleann na Péiste on the way?'

'It's fairly hard to find. It's well off the track. Do you know . . .?' I didn't. 'Do you know . . . ?' After naming nearly half-a-dozen rocks and ditches, I was still none the wiser. I knew none of them, yet it was evident to Sue that I was not going to give up. 'Right, I don't think you'll find it this way, but climb up to the fort. From there, look down to the southern cliffs and you'll spot a long bank or ditch. Walk straight down to that and follow it to the west. You can't miss the rock. It's a huge, almost flat, slab, covered with names and dates. I haven't seen it in a while, so it may be covered in lichen again and hard to read.'

My mission was sealed. I set off back the road with a purpose. Two stonechats flew along the cliff line on my left, threading together the tufts of heather. They matched my progress as far as the crossroads. As the hill fell away on my right, Inis Tuaisceart or *An Fear Marbh*, as Sue had called it, came into view once more. The north wind assaulted me

Sue Redican, weaver and island matriarch.

again, and the two stonechats retreated to the sheltered southern path. I repeated Sue's directions in my mind and began the slippery ascent to the fort with the wind whistling in my ears. I scanned the southern cliffs looking for the rock as I climbed. There were hundreds of standing rocks of huge proportions in the valley below. Still, I was convinced that I would be able to spot it from the fort.

I kept low on my hands and knees as the gale whipped over the cliff. To my left, the pyramid-shaped island of An Téaracht came in view. In seconds, a grey squall of horizontal rain swept over it and it disappeared from view again. I crouched down in the remains of what looked like a beehive hut. My ears were ringing from the noise of the wind. From there, I contemplated the southern slopes, a continuum of rises and falls, full of turf banks and littered with every make and shape of rock. Sue had also said that Gleann na Péiste overlooked a horseshoe-shaped cove, Cladach na gCapall. I looked in desperation. The whole cliff line was indented with bites. I chose a rock that stood defiant and taller than the rest, and made that my target.

As I went over the top of the fort, the wind whipped around me from all sides and the rain was like shrapnel in my face. I focused on the rock and walked, the slope pulling me down faster than I could manage. I sank knee-deep in heather and fell into rabbit holes. As I looked back up the slope into the wind, the path home seemed an impossible distance away. I was covered in brown bog-water up to my thighs. The rock I reached looked no different from the others: the eroded lunar landscape of the clifftop was littered with them. I wandered around this natural Stonehenge. Several times the gale blew me over. I sheltered behind a rock, ate half my scone and conducted a serious inquiry as to what I was doing there: the answer was that Páidí Dunleavy had dragged me there and Páidí Dunleavy I was going to find!

Looking for one particular rock amongst three miles of rock was proving to be a ridiculous task. The bank that Sue had mentioned turned out to be just as elusive. Both the bank and the path that Páidí Dunleavy had trod were well obscured by years of growth.

I began to follow the coastline westwards, keeping as far back from the edge as possible. Suddenly, I could see the outline of the cliff gathered in under the slopes, like a skirt revealing a sparkling blue petticoat. A hundred and fifty metres below me lay the horseshoe-shaped bay with a lush balcony tucked into the slopes high above the cliffs: I had found Gleann na Péiste. Creeping buttercups and lush ferns thrived in this south-facing garden, a haven of peace and greenery, in contrast to the wind-burnt heather and bracken not far away.

I dropped my backpack and wandered around as far as I could on the old cart path, looking for the stone. There was none – it was by far the lushest part of the island I had seen yet. When I returned to my bag, two rabbits were having a good snoop. 'Do you mind?' Neither of them seemed particularly bothered until I picked up my bag and they lolloped off, eyeing me from a convenient burrow. I peeled a banana and sat back against the warm rock face, relishing the peace and shelter from the wind.

I thought about Páidí Dunleavy and the hundreds of islanders who had hauled turf along the path in Gleann na Péiste over the years. 'Life is tough but you get on with it.' Basking in the sunshine, I watched gulls rise on elevators of air. I sang for myself and my new-found freedom, for the gulls, for the rabbits, for Páidí Dunleavy. I had not found the stone, but I was as contented as if I had. I hauled myself up, scattering my rabbit audience in all directions. As I bent down to retrieve my bag, I suddenly spotted it: 'Páidí Dunleavy.'

The name was followed by a carved series of dates ranging from the 1960s to the early 1990s. Although speckled with lichen, the deep cuts in the rock ensured that Páidí's name remained for posterity. Ironically, as soon as I had given up the search, it was Páidí's rock I had sat back on. He would have had a good laugh about that. It was a flat wall of rock. Through the orange and black lichen stains, the names of dozens of Blasket Islanders announced themselves. On the bottom right of the rock face was the name of Páidí Dunleavy. After that there was nowhere else to write. It was as if Páidí had finished the page.

The Three Shepherds

I walked the ridge tiles of the world every day. On my right the island tumbled down into the muffled roar. On my left, the cliffs disappeared into a sea of shimmering Chinese silk, stretching as far as the pyramid-shaped Skelligs on the southern horizon. I followed the spine of the island, up to the fort, down along the saddle, up and over An Cró, then descending the Red Ridge (Drom Rua Chráilí) to the most westerly tip known as Black Head (An Ceann Dubh). There was nothing between there and the next parish of America except three thousand miles of Atlantic Ocean and the uninhabited islands of Inis na Bró, An Téaracht and Inis Mhic Uibhleain.

I settled down among the crumpled ruins of a beehive hut, out of the rush of the wind, training the binoculars on some passing gannets. The birds' vast wingspans sliced through the air. Strange that they never landed on the Great Blasket Island. Already they were miles from their huge colony on the Skelligs.

In the background was Inis Mhic Uibhleain, owned by former Taoiseach Charles Haughey. I had never seen anybody on it until that day. A lone figure walked from the house up to the jagged heights in the centre of the island. Like the

The Red Ridge on the Great Blasket Island.

monastic ruins in the centre of the island, the stone house blended into the landscape. The figure, too, merged in with the landscape, discernible only through its movement. Once up against the skyline, its silhouette merged with the standing stones and was gone. I wondered what kind of man would retreat to the uninhabited harshness of that barren landscape.

As I ambled back to the village, I wondered if people speculated about the type of woman it was who would choose to live alone in a leaking cowshed on the Great Blasket Island. Whatever our respective reasons, I felt an affinity with that lone figure on the hill.

It was evening before I got back to the village. Sue had left a note under a stone by the door. '*Seascapes* is on the radio at 7 p.m. Come down!' I could hardly believe that it was Thursday again. A whole week had passed since the day I had found Páidí's rock. I ate dinner and headed down the path. Tom MacSweeney's weekly greeting 'to this island nation' had never seemed so relevant. Thanks to the north wind and no ferries, our island nation still consisted of two inhabitants, Sue and me. I ran the last few steps and leaped up onto the bank outside her door. Immediately, I heard voices coming from inside. I was stunned. My first instinct was to turn around and get away, but it was too late: Sue had spotted me.

When I entered, three men greeted me in Irish. I smiled nervously but could not say a word. As the conversation proceeded, my lack of comprehension was painfully obvious. Tactfully, they switched to English. 'And what country are you from?' asked one of the men. For the first time in my life I felt utterly ashamed of my lack of Irish. I couldn't string together even a simple sentence.

It turned out that each of the three men owned sheep on the island. Although their families had abandoned the island more then a half a century before, they continued to return every year, just like their grandfathers and fathers had done, to rear sheep for sale in the market in Dingle. They also grazed eighty sheep on Inis Tuaisceart. I had read about the difficulties of landing and scaling the cliffs on Inis Tuaisceart, so I could not imagine how eighty sheep would be hauled up onto the island. I wanted to ask them how they managed it, but couldn't. Acutely aware of having interrupted the flow of their Irish conversation and feeling even more awkward, I seized my opportunity to say goodnight as Sue began to serve up dinner. On the way back home, I had to walk around several large fish boxes piled high with sleeping bags, a stove, gas, sliced bread, batteries, cans of beer and shears. As I looked at the stuff piled high, I wondered anxiously if I was living in the place where the men usually stayed.

Next morning, the startling sound of barking dogs and the shouting of urgent commands filled the hut. Unlike me, even the dogs understood Irish. I sat up and peered out of my tiny window as an orderly procession of sheep shuffled along the lower path through the ruins. Two young dogs wheeled around them in wide circles, panting and barking. An old dog worried the heels of the last sheep and, with the slightest dip to right or left, he directed the flock into a wooden pen above the beach.

That evening as I rounded An Gob on my way home, I was greeted by the bawling of sheep. The pen below was a heaving mass of wool. Two of the men were hammering stakes into the ground. The smell of wood smoke from Sue's chimney carried on the wind: she had lit the fire early. Seeing the men busy at work, I cut straight down the hillside to her house. One of the sheepdogs lay outside her door, its head resting on the worn step. He barely glanced at me, exhausted after his day's labours. I patted his tired head and stepped into the dimly lit interior. 'Just in time,' Sue announced. When the darkness took shape, Sue stood, filling the steaming teapot on the gas stove. The table was laden with wooden bowls, platters and candleholders. By the fire sat one of the sheep men. As he looked up, I was struck by the startling blue of his eyes.

'I'm sorry, Sue – I didn't realise you had company. Just called to tell you I saw the falcons again.'

'Sit down. Páid and I are just about to have tea. You're always in a terrible hurry. Mind you, you've slowed down a bit, but you've still a way to go.' I sat down and smiled. I didn't know quite how to react to that statement. As I looked at the fire to hide my embarrassment, I thought how right she was. Páid said nothing, and just looked at the fire too as Sue settled the teapot and three mugs on the hearth. 'So where did you spot them, Anita?'

'I was up in the fort, leaning against the bank, when one of them came sailing overhead. It passed over westwards, then began hovering over a spot about fifty yards away. It stayed in the same spot for at least ten minutes, then suddenly folded in its wings and plummeted like a stone. I could hear it cry once or twice and then the second one joined it.'

'It must have killed a rabbit. It's only recently that they've come back to the island. They were nearly extinct all over the country because of DDT. It used to make the eggshells soft and so the chicks died,' Sue explained.

'I see them when I'm lifting pots off the Lóchar Rocks.' It was the first time Páid had spoken. He had a very attractive, gentle voice. Immediately, I recalled the small boat I had seen at the Lóchar Rocks, thrashing violently in the waves, 300 metres below the fort, three days previously. In it had been a lone fisherman in yellow oilskins. I had not been able to take my eyes off the toy vessel and the tiny man throwing lobster pots over the side. My imagination had played out the disaster. I would be the only witness. It would take me at least half an hour to get back around to Sue's to radio for help. Then the lifeboat from Valentia would take, what? Another two hours? He would be dashed to pieces on the rocks. I had given myself palpitations imagining every possible scenario. I could not believe that he would go out in a tiny boat when even the ferries were not running. Mind you, the three of them had crossed into the island when no other boats dared. 'I think I saw you lifting pots at the Lóchar Rocks on Tuesday' was all I dared to contribute from the extensive search-and-rescue plan that was replaying in my head.

'That you did', he replied and we both continued to stare at the fire.

Sue poured the tea. 'Páid does woodcarving in the winter and I sell his work here in on the island.'

When the conversation turned to wood, Páid became animated, showing us unusual grains and telling us how to distinguish the different woods. We took it in turns to stroke the grain of ash, cherry, oak and sycamore. Soon, the floor was covered with as much wood as wool. Sue poured more tea. 'Is it time to make tea for Páid yet, do you think?' she asked.

'It is, he should be up shortly,' Páid said.

'Sorry, I thought that your name was Páid,' I said.

'It is, but the other man is Páid too.'

Sue came to the rescue and explained. 'We call the other man Páidí. Páidí Kearney.'

Just then Páidí Kearney came in the door, followed by his old sheepdog. Páid pushed him a small milking stool with his foot and said something in Irish. Páidí Kearney then looked at me and smiled. 'All good I hope.'

'No, no we weren't talking *about* you,' I hastened to add. 'I was just trying to get your names right.'

'Oh sure now, you have me disappointed.' I was still very anxious with people in general, but a lot less so with the people of the island. Páidí Kearney put me at my ease immediately.

'Have you any connections with the island?' I asked him.

'My people come from the Great Blasket Island. My uncle was Seán Kearney and he lived and died in the Kearney family home, just below the schoolhouse. It was because of his death that everyone finally abandoned the island.' Before he could explain any more, the third man, Donncha, arrived in. I began to make my exit.

'And why does the whole island population leave when I come in?' he asked loudly as he blocked the doorway. What followed was the third degree: my name, where I came from and what I was doing staying in on the island alone.

'You must be either a nun or a hermit. Are you a member of one of those cults?' he continued. I was getting desperate. Why couldn't I think of an answer to deflect this interrogation? Why could I never come up with the kind of witty, clever jibes that seemed to skip effortlessly off other peoples' tongues? Páidí came to my rescue several times by changing the conversation.

'Ah, Sue, I forgot,' Páidí interrupted as he delved into a small haversack on the floor and produced a bottle of wine, a present from his wife who worked in the craft shop in Ballyferriter on the Dingle Peninsula. Talk turned to Páidí's work. Like Páid, he too had a craft. He was a master potter with Louis Mulcahy.

'So, you are both fishermen, sheep farmers and crafts-men!' I was fascinated and envious.

'Everyone has to be involved in the tourist industry here – bed and breakfasts, restaurants, crafts. What else is there on the peninsula? The bit of fishing and sheep farming we do wouldn't keep anybody alive. Sure that's why they all had to emigrate in the past,' Páidí explained.

'Not like the wealthy farmers and nuns in County Kilkenny, eh?' laughed Donncha. Maybe agreeing with him might help to stop the teasing. I pretended to laugh with him. Sue offered me a glass of wine. I declined. It was time to leave.

'I knew it. She's in a cult. She doesn't drink either.' I thanked Sue, ignoring the ribbing. As politely as I could, I edged towards the door.

'I wouldn't like to be going up there in the dark on my own. Ray's place is haunted, isn't it, Páidí?' laughed Donncha.

'It isn't. It's outside that's haunted,' I said quietly, looking him in the eye. For the first time, I had managed to stop his banter stone dead. Instantly, I was sorry that I had said anything. I had exposed myself to ridicule, yet I was anxious for confirmation. Confirmation that I wasn't going mad. Sue and each of the three men had heard various accounts of haunting over the years. Up around the cafe, they all agreed, was one area on the island that was definitely haunted. Each of the men had stories to tell but most were disregarded with the addendum 'sure he had a skinful that night.' Páidí mentioned voices in the darkness heard up at Tobar na Croise, the well outside my hut.

It was then that I told the men and Sue of the chatter and laughter each night at the beginning of my stay. I told them about the two little girls and about how it had never crossed my mind that they were anybody other then the children of the ferrymen or the couple in the cafe. After discussing my story, they concluded that the voices heard at the well by others must have been the spirits of the children I had seen.

'But why should a stranger on the island be the first to see them?' Donncha asked. I began to feel that I was on trial.

'Well, you're a teacher, aren't you?' Páidí said. 'You're obviously good with kids. They wanted you to see them, and maybe they wanted you to go into the old school with them.'

Sue and the men were surprised at my certainty that I

would not see the children again. As I said it aloud, I knew how true it was. When layers of one's being are shaken and stripped to the core, perhaps the spirit is exposed. I knew that it was on that deeper level that I had met the spirits of the two girls. If other people had been with me on those nights, perhaps they would have seen nothing, being physically stronger and more spiritually fortified than I was. I began to realise that it was with my soul's eyes and not my physical eyes that I had seen the girls on those tortured nights. That desperate time had now passed for me, and I knew that I had become physically and emotionally stronger. If the two little girls were a symptom of my distress, they were also a remedy for that distress. As I left, Sue and the men were still discussing what I had seen.

The following morning, the men began shearing the sheep in the wooden pen. Páid waded into the bleating sea of wool, selecting the next fleece. In seconds, the terrified ewe was upended and her fleece peeled off her as easily as fleshy skin is peeled off an orange. Exposed in her velvety white under-flesh, she hobbled back into the flock for cover. Her woolly companions wheeled around and around in the enclosure as Páid lunged after new victims. The young dogs barked excitedly, but after one sharp command in Irish, they dropped to the ground like stones. As a mountain of fleeces piled up out on the grass, in the pen the flock became skinnier and whiter by the hour.

The noise and the activity were so reminiscent of my childhood that I lingered around the hut all morning. After cleaning the floor with my improvised heather broom, I heated water on the stove and washed some clothes in a basin while sitting against the wall of the *Dáil*, protected from the north wind. Then it was time for a cup of tea. I negotiated the banks and rabbit holes down to the sheep pen, gripping four steaming mugs. The men leaned back on the bleached wooden fence against a backdrop of brilliant blue sea and sky. 'Well, she still has no Irish but she makes a great cup of tea,' Páidí announced.

'At least that's one tradition these wealthy Kilkenny farmers haven't thrown out the window along with everything else,' Donncha teased.

Startled by the loud talk and sudden bursts of laughter, the sheep huddled against the far side of the pen.

That evening, after the sun had gone down, the stories continued at Sue's fireside. Donncha had gone back out to the mainland and his place had been taken by a quiet, gentle, weather-beaten man called Séamus.

The shearing took four days. The wool was gathered and stored in the dry *clochán* in front of Páidí Dunleavy's. On the final afternoon, Sue and I were roped in to help. We herded the sheep down the cliff to the slipway where Páid manoeuvred the small boat so that Séamus and Páidí could catch each animal, haul it into the boat and tie its legs together. When the cargo of twelve sheep was finally aboard, they set off for Beiginis, where the grazing was rich and they could be fattened for a couple of weeks before their final journey across the Blasket Sound and into Dingle, to be sold as organic Blasket lamb to upmarket restaurants.

As the day passed, the flock got smaller on the slipway. I made several pots of tea and took turns blocking the flock's escape route back up the cliff. The task of lifting each animal was arduous and physically exhausting. As the little boat returned from Beiginis, another ewe would be unceremoni- ously upended, and her legs tied as she bleated pitifully. 'Why do you have to tie their legs together?' I asked.

'Because they'd jump overboard,' Páidí explained.

'Sure, they huddle in the middle of the boat, terrified the whole way over,' Páid argued. 'When did you ever hear of a

Séamus with his sheepdogs at the slipway.

ewe diving in for a swim?' The two men stood up in the boat debating the question.

After a time, Séamus, the quietest of the three, spoke. 'It's to stop them putting their hooves through the canvas and sinking the currach.' There was silence for a time.

'Sure we have solid floors wit' years, we're not shifting them in currachs any more,' Páid said.

The rhythm of the work was interrupted as we all silently contemplated the bound ewe on the solid floor of the boat.

Then Páidí spoke. 'I suppose some of the old ways don't make sense any more.'

With that, we watched Páidí untie the ewe that cowered in the bottom of the boat.

At dusk, I sat with Séamus and the sheepdogs on the rocks watching the last boat of unbound sheep crossing to Beiginis. As I watched, I felt guilty.

'With one question I've just destroyed an age-old, vibrant Blasket tradition.'

Séamus continued to look out to sea as he nodded, then turned to me smiling, 'Sure, with a cup of tea from an island house, didn't you revive another?'

Manslaughter

The stories told at Sue's fireside filled my imagination and became my salvation. The obsessive replaying of memories in all their forensic detail lessened as I walked the island living these new tales. Much of the folklore related to the fishermen and seals of the islands. The story of Muiris and the seal is one such Blasket legend.

A fisherman on the Great Blasket Island, Muiris was renowned as far away as Dingle for the heavy catches he netted. When hauls were meagre for everyone else, Muiris's nets were always guaranteed to be full. Some said it was because he had been born on the Feast Day of Saints Peter and Paul. Others said that it was the old seal that had followed his boat constantly since the night his father had drowned which brought him luck. Whatever the reason, islanders said it was lucky to run your hand along the bow of Muiris's boat: that hand would be promised plenty. It was said that a Dingle woman who had no children ran her hands along the boat and, nine months later, she was cradling a son in her arms. Muiris himself knew the secret of his laden nets, but he also knew that to speak about that secret would break the spell forever.

Muiris had been a rival, along with his friend Tomás, for the affections of a young island girl called Úna. Eighteen years old, with long auburn hair to her waist, she had sparkling eyes of liquid sea blue. Muiris and Tomás approached her father, seeking her hand in marriage, within days of each other. Úna, who had strong views of her own, favoured Muiris. The wedding took place in Ballyferriter and then Úna moved into the neat little house of Muiris and his widowed mother on the Great Blasket Island. The couple were as happy as larks and the two women got on famously.

Tomás, on the other hand, was anything but happy, and could not let go of his bitterness and jealousy, which festered like an infected sore. One calm evening, as the boats were gliding through the sea back home to the island, Tomás had only a few mackerel to show for his full day's fishing. In contrast, Muiris's boat was low in the water, such was the weight of his catch. Tomás was consumed with resentment. He thought of Úna, and his knuckles clenched white on the oars.

It was just as Tomás was approaching the head of *An Fear Marbh* that he caught sight of the old seal gliding back through the waves, having left Muiris at the Great Blasket Island. In an instant the young man took his revenge. As the old seal passed by, he brought down the oar on its head with all the anger and hate he could muster, cracking open the creature's skull. It rolled over in the water, limp and dead. Tomás towed the seal back to the island where he stowed it out of sight, below the slipway.

It was late and dark when he returned to the hiding place and hauled the shiny black body back to his cottage. He rolled it into the turf shed and covered it with sods. He would make use of every ounce of meat, blubber and skin. In cold and frosty weather, it would hold well.

Manslaughter

The next day the boats went out again. Muiris waited in vain for the sleek black head to bob up beside him. He fished all day and, for the first time in ten years, came home with an empty boat. The village was wild with talk. 'The seal has deserted Muiris and so has his luck.'

'Nothing will go right for him now, Lord bless the lad!'

Muiris felt as bereft as when his father had died all those years before. He went out in the boat the next day and the one after that, waiting, watching and scanning the tide desperately for the seal. On the third day, the weather broke and the wind scuffed white peaks across the water. The other men worked at hauling turf and mending nets, instead of putting out to sea. But Muiris had other plans. Too late, Úna discovered those plans: Muiris was already pushing the boat out into the waves. She pleaded with him not to go. He ignored her and shouted that he had to find the seal.

All day Úna stood on the cliffs above the seal cove, waiting for Muiris to return. She stared at the waves crashing against the rocky head of *An Fear Marbh*, praying to the Virgin to send him home safely. When darkness fell, her mother-in-law continued the vigil with her. She understood the pain of waiting. For ten years she had watched for her own husband to return from the sea and now she would have to watch for her son. The two women never moved until dawn, when neighbours came to take them home. The search of the shoreline began because it was still too rough for a boat to risk venturing out. All day the islanders watched, waited and searched. There was no trace of Muiris or his boat.

As darkness fell, a storm raged over the island. The waves dashed themselves against the rocks, shattering into plumes of spray. Doors and windows were shuttered against the wind and the driving rain. The whole village lay awake listening to the voices of a hundred seals wailing and crying in the darkness.

Their howling reverberated throughout the village: nothing like it has been heard on the island before or since.

In his cottage Tomás and his two sisters, Máire and Cáit, sat up beside the fire for comfort. The wind blew smoke back down the chimney until it eventually put out the fire. The wailing of the seals was relentless. Tomás was uneasy. Beads of sweat shone on his upper lip. He began pacing incessantly between the window and the hearth.

'For the love of God, Tomás, will you sit down and stop yer fidgeting!'

'Can't ye hear that?' he snapped.

''Tis only the seals. Sure they're unsettled by the storm too.'

Tomás was not consoled. He was terrified. The wails sent shivers of fear through him. He grabbed the chamberpot, sprinkling stale urine at the window, the door and the hearth and then in the corners of the house, for protection.

'Can't ye hear them getting closer?' The sisters continued to try to soothe him, but his growing panic was making them uneasy too. He was right. It *did* sound as if the wailing was getting nearer. Soon, a long, deep-throated wail rose from just outside the house. Tomás squatted at the hearth, his head in his hands, his body convulsed in terror. 'Jesus, Mary and Joseph, protect me.'

'Tomás, what is it? What have you done?' cried Cáit.

'I killed the seal, I killed Muiris's seal and hid it in the turf.' The sisters now looked mortally afraid. Another wail rose from just outside, followed quickly by knocking on the door of the house. Tomás jumped in fright.

'You've got to open it, Tomás,' urged Máire. He shook his head, weeping.

Máire lifted the latch and opened the door. As she did, the lamplight reflected off the glistening coats of six female seals. From their huge black eyes rivers of brine spilled down their faces. They stared past the sisters, holding Tomás in their gaze, all the while forming a path in the darkness to the turf shed. Tomás was compelled to follow them.

The islanders who witnessed what followed said it was the strangest sight that ever was seen on the island. A funeral procession of six wailing seals lumbering down Bóthar na Marbh, followed by Tómas dragging a dead seal. The seals made slow progress through the village, their desolate cries wrenching the hearts of all who heard them. Tomás followed them right down onto the White Strand, where the sand was a writhing mass of seals. As the procession of six seals advanced, the herd parted before them, then regrouped, absorbing them into its midst. The keening of the seals lasted right through the night, until it seemed that the very heart of the island was engulfed in grief.

Just before dawn, the lament suddenly stopped: the ensuing eerie silence was as chilling as the wailing. As the whiteness of dawn seeped over the horizon, the islanders lined the clifftop ready to resume the search for Muiris. Layers of darkness evaporated, exposing an extraordinary sight below them: over two hundred black, grey and dappled seals formed a great circular mass on the beach, all straining towards the centre of the herd.

Gradually, the approaching weak rays of sunlight moved over the sand and the seals. As if on cue, six older cows turned away and glided into the incoming tide. Breaking ranks, the others followed, rippling into the waves, silently.

A huge circular area of dark, churned sand remained. In the centre lay two motionless shapes. The islanders too stayed immobile for a time until one individual took the lead and began to edge his way down the cliff. Suddenly, everyone began to slide and scamper down the cliff and run across the beach. On the wet sand lay two human corpses: the drowned remains of young Muiris and, beside him, the drowned remains of his father Seán, his skull cracked open from a blow to the head.

Úna and her mother-in-law had the corpses of their husbands carried up to their house, where they were laid out on the kitchen table on a white cloth, as was the old custom. Above the corpses, the corners of a white sheet were tied to the rafters, forming a canopy, and on each of the corners of the table burned a candle. The two widows sat up keening the corpses for two nights. As the island waked Muiris, dead for three days and Seán, dead for ten years, six seals patrolled offshore day and night. Only after the bodies of the men were taken out to the mainland for burial did the seals finally disappear.

Tomás was never seen again after the funerals of Muiris and Seán. Some said he went to America; some said he went to Dingle; others said that only the seals knew his fate.

The Normandy Landing

Sue was busy baking. Two trays of hot, golden scones cooled on a wire tray. My mouth had begun watering within twenty yards of her door, as I smelled them on the way back from my morning swim.

'Well, make the tea and put one of them out of their misery,' Sue said as she looked up from the mixing bowl. I put the kettle on the stove and told her that there was no sign of the men and that the boat was gone.

'It's gone about four hours at this stage. The lads were knocking at the door looking for a cup of tea at six o'clock this morning.'

I felt quite lonely. I would miss their company, their stories and their old sheepdog. 'The ferries are back on today,' Sue continued. 'The forecast is good for the week. Unless Seán is bringing in fresh baking from Dingle, the hordes will all be descending on me for a cup of tea.'

Feeling aggrieved at the unexpected departure of the men, the significance of what Sue was talking about was lost on me. Today had begun like every other day, with a freezing swim on the White Strand, watched by the Beverley Sisters, followed by a walk along the strand. The only difference between today and previous days was the weather, an azure blue sea with a gleaming jade Beiginis, the air still and warm. Already, the stone wall around Sue's little courtyard was heating up from the sun's rays. I sat there, enjoying my tea and hot scone as Sue got on with her preparations. Once the baking was finished, she lifted her spinning wheel onto the low wall and hung a large, wooden shop sign on two rusty nails on the gable wall. Sugar and milk were placed on an upturned box in the centre of the courtyard and the Weaver's Shop and Cafe was open for business.

I strolled back up to my hut and resumed my daily routine. I shook out my sleeping bag, swept the sand and remains of Mr Robin's breakfast out the door, got water from the well, put the porridge on the stove. I gathered up the carrot and potato peelings from the previous evening and shared them out at the entrances to the busiest rabbit holes.

Once the porridge was ready, I settled myself onto my sheepskin fleece on the chair in the sunshine. Sue had given me a cup of sugar. I marvelled as it melted over the porridge, forming a sweet clear liquid between the porridge and the inside of the bowl. So entranced was I by the sheer luxury of this morning's breakfast that I didn't see the ferries setting off from Dún Chaoin.

The red ferry was almost in to the island. The blue followed. Both were laden with tourists and towed dinghies. Cameras and binoculars were trained up into the ruined village. Suddenly I felt self-conscious and retreated inside to eat my food. From the tiny window I could see the first heads appearing over the top of the cliff. A blaze of coloured shorts and Day-Glo jackets scattered between the ruins. Many struggled up the hill at a snail's pace, stopping to rest on walls or just to straighten up. Seán and Laura stood out from the tourists. They bolted across the low path like two goats, despite the weight of their supplies for the hostel.

Sitting outside Ray Stagle's cowshed in the sunshine.

Dinghy-load after dinghy-load of day-trippers landed and came over the top of the cliff. They began their exploration of the village. They fanned out and combed every stone and ruin searching for the ideal photograph or memento. As they advanced, another group followed. There were probably fifty in the first wave.

I expected someone to shout suddenly 'I've found it,' and all would run to see, or perhaps 'I've found her,' and I would be discovered.

I could hear voices approach along the path. They sounded young and they sounded Spanish. A group of about fifteen teenagers ambled along the path below the hut. A mobile phone rang and the boy who answered began arguing loudly. As they passed up the hill outside my hut, I could see their legs. I willed them to keep moving. Suddenly, two boys ran up the bank to my door. One boy stepped inside as the other put his head in under the lintel. They looked around and shouted down to their friends in Spanish, presumably reporting their discovery and then they ducked back out again. They never said a word to me, never acknowledged my presence. More legs stopped and more heads bent down to have a look in. My heart began to pound.

Two huge American women flopped down on the bank beside the well. 'Look, Gloria, there's water in the tap. You think it's safe to drink it?' Even from a distance, her voice was loud and grating.

'Don't, honey. That water is coming straight out of the ground. It ain't even purified.' They opted for a can of Coke out of their backpack instead. I wondered how the islanders had survived for thousands of years on pure spring water, deprived of fluoride and chlorine. As Gloria and her friend broadcast to the island details of their latest detox programme, a young boy pressed his face to my tiny window. 'Look, Dad, there's a woman in here.' He continued to stare at me until 'Dad' came to confirm his find. I pretended not to notice them and continued to stare at my book.

'Is this a museum?' The man was in my house before I could stop him. He picked up one of my drawings.

'No, this is private. Sorry.' I grabbed my drawing from him and he looked at me, annoyed.

'Well, you should have "private" on the door then.'

When he left, I closed the door and pulled the bolt across. Between the door and the lintel there was at least a one-inch gap of daylight. For every ten tourists who passed, one would present a huge eye to the chink and rattle the door. I was sure someone would push it in. I felt under siege, claustrophobic. Suddenly, there was a bright flash as a camera whirred against the glass of the tiny window. A wave of nausea surged through me from the pit of my stomach. I pushed two corners of the dishcloth between the stones above the window and let the cloth fall like a curtain. I grabbed the old blanket and put it in its windbreak position across the door.

Gasping for breath, I sat on the bunk shaking. My chest tightened. The old feelings of fear and helplessness were back. They seemed to take control of me again, but for the first time there was some part of me that was aware of them and disengaged from their assault. I clung on, focusing all my attention on the blanket. I did not black out. It was at that point that I realised how much I had healed since my encounter with the two little girls. They had plunged their hands inside a hellish bleeding wound and had found me. They had pulled me out and restored me to safety. I looked at my trembling hands and legs and resolved that I was not going back there again, ever.

Such irony – there I was witnessing the first calm, sunny day on that beautiful island in almost two weeks, and I was barricaded in my hut for almost three hours. In a huge bid to regain control, I began to look at my options. It was too late to head to the back of the island. Sitting outside was also impossible. People would stop and want to talk to me. I filled a bottle of water from the saucepan, wrapped Sue's three-day-old scone in a sheet of writing paper and placed the water, the scone and a book in my backpack. I watched through the crack in the door for a break in the line of sightseers and then hurried out, pulling my towel off my makeshift clothes line as I went. Without a sideways glance, I set off. By then, I could have found my way blindfolded to the beach, dodging effort-lessly every rabbit hole and nettle. A group of middle-aged English walkers marched up the path, armed with walking poles, sturdy boots and gaiters, compasses and laminated maps around their necks. Each one also carried an enormous back-pack. Two of the female walkers scanned me disapprovingly as I sped by. I heard the word 'hippie' being uttered as I passed. Then it occurred to me that I had not looked in a mirror in over two weeks. What did they see? Bare feet and bare legs under a torn jungle shirt, and tangled long hair that had not been exposed to anything but sea water, wind and salt since my arrival. I headed straight for the beach, confirming all their suspicions.

The beach was packed with tourists. People sat side by side on the sand, not acknowledging each other's existence. It reminded me of being on the tube in London, where people manage to create their own self-contained bubble inches from another person's face. In the most crowded place on the island, the beach, I found the most privacy. Nobody would invade my space here, pick up my journal, or take photos of me as if I was a museum piece. I sat back against the warm rock, forcing deep, calm breaths into my lungs. My feet were coated with hot, white sand. I opened the book on my lap and watched the activity from under the sanctuary of my hat. The Great Blasket Island seemed like a different place. Gone were the rain, the cold sand and the Beverley Sisters. In their stead were a South Pacific island, sparkling blue sea and dazzling white sand. A group of children fought valiantly against the incoming tide as it dissolved their sandcastle walls. Some American university students sat and lay around their tutor farther along the beach. Gradually, they peeled away from their tutorial, tempted by the allure of a yellow frisbee. Couples of various nationalities strolled along the tideline. An assortment of white male stomachs ballooned from the sand at intervals. Families and couples crowded the beach, all observing invisible boundaries that shielded them from their neighbours. The father and son who had barged in on me earlier came and sat against the rocks a few feet from me. I looked over. Both of them failed to acknowledge my presence now.

During the afternoon the ferries ploughed relentlessly between the mainland and the island. Clusters of purposeful day-trippers landed and launched fresh waves of attack. As I paddled in the ripples, I looked up at the island. Most people in these landing parties seemed to follow exactly the same well-trodden routes – to the weaver's house, the cafe and the toilet between the hostel and the cafe. Many ignored the climb up into the village and headed straight to the beach. Large groups were gathered outside the cafe on picnic benches, while a constantly changing gathering rested itself outside Sue's door. Many, on leaving Sue's house, stopped and orientated themselves by opening out large maps. They too followed well-worn paths that led them to the ruined homes of the island writers – Tomás Ó Croimhthain, Muiris Ó Súilleabháin – and, eventually, up to the hostel, which had once been the home of the legendary Peig Sayers. From there, most went next door to the cafe, once home to an islander known as the Buffer Keane, where they sat and watched for the return ferry.

Some individuals – though very few – seemed to step ashore with no predetermined plan. They ambled, allowing the island to unfold before them, wandering off the beaten track. One or two beat their way through the heather and bracken, heading straight to the top of the island. My heart lifted in anticipation of the thrill that awaited them: the islands to the west, the Sleeping Giant of Inis Tuaisceart to the north and the hazy pyramids of the Skelligs on the southern horizon. Each of these people, in their turn, stared and was still for a long time.

Gradually the returning ferries drew the people from the cafe, the beach and the hillside. They spilled down through the village like an ebbing wave. The beach began to empty and I dragged my towel farther down as the shadow slipped across the rocks.

A couple on front of me waited until the last minute. 'We'll miss it if we don't go now. The children will be wondering where we've got to.' The woman had her bag over her shoulder and stood waiting for her husband.

'You'll only be standing there waiting like the rest of them. It won't go on time. Sit down.' The man lay on the sand, his inflated stomach a nasty shade of pink.

'The ferryman said half four. The blue ferry tickets return at half four.' She stood there holding his shirt out to him. He ignored the shirt.

'Look, he'll say that to everyone so as to make sure that they're all not going to turn up for the last ferry. Sit down or move. You're in my sun.'

'You know more than the ferryman then, do you? Well, maybe *you* don't mind leaving the children on their own in Dingle for the night, but I do.' With that, she flung the shirt onto his stomach and charged up the beach. She seemed to be bitter and angry. I wondered was it years of living with him that made her so? I watched the crowd on the slipway thin out as the dinghies moved in and out to the waiting ferries. A bit of me willed him to miss it, to make him pay for dismissing his wife's anxiety. It was only when the last remaining dinghy made for the slipway that he moved. He waddled up the beach casually.

I watched the last ferry disappear and, with it, the tension in my body. As my shoulders relaxed again, I was aware of how rigid they had been all day. I took off my hat and stretched out in the sand. The sandcastles had long since been swallowed up by the incoming tide and the waves dissolved and smoothed the footprints of hundreds of people. As I walked back up to the rocks, I saw a plastic bottle on the sand. I stared at it for a minute, then picked it up. I had no idea what I was going to do with it. After that, I spotted a crisp bag, another plastic bottle and a chocolate wrapper. Another wave broke and a plastic supermarket bag was sucked back into the sea. I imagined one of the seals choking on it. The water was up to my thighs before I managed to retrieve it.

Laden with plastic rubbish, I struggled back up the cliff and into the lower village. Like someone returning to a former war zone, I was still cautious, on the lookout for a remaining sniper wielding a camera. I thought of my hut and wondered if the door had been pushed in. I tried to quicken my pace back up through the ruins, but my knees were still too weak. The various shocks of the day were quickly turning to anger and upset. How was I going to face this every day? Why could I not just get on with it like everyone else? So preoccupied was I that I did not see Sue coming along the path.

'Well, don't you look a sight!' she said. I could have said the same to her. She also was clutching an assortment of plastic wrappers and a cracked yellow frisbee. 'So how did you survive the Normandy Landing?'

Cannibals

It was a week later in the early morning. Sue was returning from her walk to meet the first ferryload of tourists and to open up her shop. I was escaping to the back of the island and had just locked my door. We met each other halfway along the north path. 'They must be on their way, judging by the speed of you,' she smiled.

'Yes, first ferry has just set off. You've got twenty minutes at least before they arrive.'

'I'd gladly swop with you today. It's beautiful at the back of the island. You don't fancy a day in the shop?' She smiled as she said it, knowing it would be my idea of hell. As soon as the first ferry set off from Dún Chaoin each day, I padlocked my door and headed to the tower, the fort and the Bright Dwellings for the day, armed with my binoculars, my book and some lunch.

'I might just pass on that today, Sue.'

'It's time we had a spell of bad weather. I need a break from the ferries.'

'Are you running short of stock?' I imagined that she needed a few uninterrupted days' weaving at this stage.

'No, not at all. I need a couple of days of peace, walking

and not talking to anybody. That's what I love about the winter.' I sat back against the wall of peat and heather that rose steeply behind us. My hands sank back into spongy moss and a cluster of beautiful little blue flowers. I touched their delicate petals. 'That's milkwort,' she said. Every time I met her, she introduced me to something new. Already I was seeing bog pimpernel, meadow buttercup, tormentil and knapweed everywhere. Now I had learned another tiny plant's name.

'How do you remember the names of them all?'

'I used to bring them back to the house and then look them up in my books. I've learned the names gradually over the years, like the birds' names. Have you seen the cannibal plant?'

'The what?'

'Cannibal plant . . . well, it's called sundew. It closes as an insect lands on it and then secretes juices to digest its victim.' I obviously looked disgusted at this bit of information: it sounded like something out of a horror film. Sue laughed and began backtracking up the north path. 'They're growing up here in the bog.'

'Hang on – do I really want to see this?' I recalled a giant clam that I had seen in a film, snapping its shell closed on the legs of a diver. Sue stepped out ahead of me. I had to run to catch up. Seventeen years on the hills of the Great Blasket Island create a fitness that is not easy to emulate. I followed her cautiously up into the bog. She stopped and bent down among mounds of dew-covered moss, picking a stem of bog cotton and indicating an innocuous-looking cluster of pink flowers, with star-like pointed petals.

'Watch this.'

She gently touched the centre of the flower, which responded by closing and pulling the stem inside. I touched another with a feather. I wasn't going to risk my finger. I touched each flower and they all closed.

'Great choreography, but you'll have them all starving. I'd better get back.'

'I'll walk back with you as far as the turn, or would you prefer a bit of peace before the Normandy Landings?'

'No, come on.' We watched the skylarks spiralling above, and two determined-looking cormorants flying back in from Inis Tuaisceart. They were easily 150 metres below us, even more.

'What will you do if the island gets busier and busier?'

Sue said nothing for a moment and then stopped walking.

'I'll just move farther out ahead of them. Out to one of the other islands. I've landed on most of them with the lads over the years. I'd live on any of them . . . well, except An Téaracht – that might get a bit claustrophobic. You couldn't walk anywhere. Inis Mhic Uibhleain or Inis na Bró would be beautiful. They were both lived on over the years.'

'Whatever about Inis na Bró, I don't think Charlie Haughey would be too keen on sharing Inis Mhic Uibhleain with you!'

'And how do you know? We might be very happy.' As she laughed, she trained her binoculars on a stonechat in the heather.

'Have you ever landed on Inis Tuaisceart?'

An Fear Marbh (Dead Man) or Sleeping Giant as visitors called it, rested three miles off to our left. The slumbering man pointed his mighty feet to America and his head to the Kerry mainland. Over his belly, his hands were clasped in repose. He had no intention of going in either direction.

'I did once when they were moving sheep. At least the sheep were pulled up on ropes. I had to climb. It's hard to

Inis Tuaisceart – An Fear Marbh – *viewed from near the signal tower on the Great Blasket.*

land there and it's impossible altogether in bad weather. Anyway, I wouldn't want to spend a night on it. It was the one time I was relieved to get off an island.'

'How come?' Sue had weathered some of the most appalling storms on the Great Blasket on her own.

'Well, maybe it was because of what happened there, but I had a bad feeling and I didn't even want to go into the *clochán.*'

'I thought Páid had only made up that story just to scare me from going back up to the hut in the dark.'

'No, it's true. It was all recorded by a historian called Du Noyer. He interviewed the people just after it happened.' I was shocked.

'But didn't the lads sleep in the *clochán* when they were shearing?'

'They did,' she laughed, 'armed with a crate of beer, a lantern and a mobile phone. And they stayed awake all night. Brave men they are. I'd better run. Call in for a cup of tea later.'

We had reached the turn. She waved goodbye and sped off to her house just as the first dinghy was leaving the ferry. I made a hasty retreat back along the north path and scampered up to the fort, where I sat back against the stones and gazed across at Inis Tuaisceart. I could see the eighty sheep dotted like baby mushrooms through the bracken. The belly of the giant was covered in plum-wine patches of heather. Through the binoculars I could follow Sue's directions along rocks, heather and broken walls to the mouth of St Brendan's *clochán*, the place where it had happened.

It was 1848. Inis Tuaisceart was always used as a sheep station. Usually no more than one family lived on the desolate and windswept island. The only shelter to be found was the *clochán*, or beehive hut, built over a hollow in the earth. The underground chamber measured only 3.3 metres in diameter, and was reached by descending a number of steep steps. In the centre a fire burned constantly and the smoke escaped through a hole in the roof.

In the autumn of 1848, a couple, Tomás Ó Catháin and his wife, Peig, went to live on the island to tend the sheep. Shortly after their arrival, the weather turned bad. The boats from Dún Chaoin and the Great Blasket Island, which normally called to the isolated shepherds with supplies, news and companionship, were unable to cross to Inis Tuaisceart. All that the Great Blasket Islanders could do was to keep a watch on the constant ribbon of smoke from the *clochán* of their storm-bound neighbours. This continued, unchanged, for two weeks, until one day a child raced into *Teach an Rí* to say that there was a fire lighting on the top of Inis Tuaisceart. The Blasket village gathered on the northern cliffs and watched the distress fire of Tomás and Peig. There was no let-up in the weather to get a boat across to them. After the day that the signal fire was seen, there was no further fire. There was no smoke from the *clochán* and no sign of anybody moving on the island. All the islanders could do was pray and wait. It took another month before a *naomhóg* could make the crossing to Inis Tuaisceart. In all, the couple had been stranded for six weeks.

Three men rowed the three miles from the Great Blasket Island to Inis Tuaisceart. The talk in the boat faltered as they got closer to the island. They had no idea what trouble they would find with Tomás and Peig. There was talk of a broken ankle, a rock fall from the roof and flooding, stranded sheep, fever and even the mischief of fairies. As the men hauled themselves up the cliffs, they became even more anxious. The island looked deserted. They called out for Tomás and Peig as they made their way up the sheep path to the enclosure.

There was no response. A ewe scampered out of their way as they came up to the *clochán*. Again they shouted to the silence.

Seán was the first into the enclosure. 'In the name of God!' He stood in shock. He had seen sheep savaged by dogs before, but nothing like this. The sheepdog lay outside the entrance, surrounded by flesh, bones and blood. The grass was littered with rotting remains. The dog hardly noticed the men as she ripped the meat of a bone between her paws. The other two men stared in silence. Seán called Tomás and Peig's names again. This time, his voice began to shake. The younger man, Liam, stepped over the carnage to join him. He stopped and buckled to his knees, retching. The two other men turned and instantly recognised what he had found on the grass. In front of him was a human leg bone half-stripped of flesh.

Seán and Séamus prayed aloud at the entrance before they bent down to peer into the darkness. The steps were sticky and wet. They could see nothing. Inside the *clochán* was dark, freezing cold and rancid. Neither could breathe with the stench. They pulled their jackets up over their mouths and stood paralysed with terror at the foot of the steps. Gradually their eyes adjusted. Through the dim light from the stairway and the chimney hole, they began to see the floor of the *clochán*, which was a bloody mess of putrefying lumps of human flesh. At the end of the steps by the men's feet was what was left of Tomás Ó Catháin; a bloated torso with its limbs hacked off and missing. Séamus threw up and clambered back up the steps into the air.

Seán stared into the darkness of the far wall. He could hear what sounded like a terrified animal under the fleeces and woollen blanket. Some kind of devilish animal had done this. In a fit of rage, he ran at it and tore the cover off the creature.

It cowered there, matted hair caked to its blood-smeared face. The eyes stared out, but saw nothing. It took a while for Seán to recognise the young girl he had once danced with in Dún Chaoin. Peig Ní Chatháin lay starving, half-dead and quite mad.

She was carried off the island and nursed on the Great Blasket for many, many months. She was not aware of anything that was done for her or of anything going on around her. The islanders said that her spirit had broken away; she had not spoken since the day the men had discovered her. Feelings ran high on both the island and the mainland: everyone had their own version of what had happened between Tomás and Peig. No version painted Peig in a good light and there were some people who would have been quite prepared to take the law into their own hands.

One day, Peig's spirit returned to her and she began to see the world around her once more. As she did, she started to talk and tell her story. Nobody who heard her ever doubted the truth of what she said.

Shortly after they had arrived on the island, Tomás began to complain of sickness and dizziness. He stopped eating and became very weak. As his fever worsened, Peig still managed to get some water past his lips and he still spoke to her. When he fell into a coma, she was gripped with fear for him and lit the distress fire. She used all the turf in that blaze, but nobody came to their rescue. He took three days to die in the darkness and the cold. The loneliness and the silence engulfed her. Tomás never regained consciousness to recognise her one last time. He died, leaving her alone. The fire had been dead for three days; she had no means of lighting a candle. While he was alive, there had been the company of his breathing in the darkness. Now there was only the black silence of death as she lay by his body.

During the days that followed, she huddled in the wind and rain at the entrance, waiting and waiting for help to arrive from the Blasket. Why didn't they see her fire? Why didn't they come for her? At night, she retreated down the steps to shelter, darkness and the cold body of her dead husband. By the time ten days had passed, the body smelled badly. The stormy weather continued and Peig remained confined in the *clochán*. Finally she decided to drag the body outside. Tomás had been a heavy man, over six foot tall. Peig was slight, and greatly weakened by grief, hunger and cold. She rolled the body to the end of the steps and then began the almost impossible task of dragging his weight up the steps. Hooking her elbows under his armpits, she strained until she cried and screamed with frustration. She couldn't remember how many days she had spent trying to move the body onto the first step. It began to decompose quickly, making her retch constantly. At night, she began to imagine that it moved, spoke to her and laughed. She screamed at it to get out, but it never would. There was only one thing to do. When it went to sleep, she would take it outside in little pieces. During daylight was the only time that it lay quietly; it would be done then.

The next morning Peig took the knife and began to hack off the arms and legs. She dragged them out singly and tried to bury them, but with no strength left, she barely covered them with grass. Then, as she hacked off the second leg, she recognised it as the body of her husband. It was Tomás. She wanted to kill herself, but she could not, so she crawled in under the fleeces and waited there to die. She could not remember the men finding her, nor could she remember her first six months back in on the Great Blasket Island.

I shivered despite the sunshine as I gazed across at the *clochán* on Inis Tuaisceart. The majesty of the Dead Man, lying oblivious to the eternal dance of sun and storms in the

Atlantic Ocean was awe-inspiring, yet it made me uneasy. Sleep brought nightmares and, with those nightmares, the monster returned. I was glad of the three miles between us. How the sheep men had spent a night in that place I just could not understand. I would never go there. It was preferable to admire it from a distance under the warmth of the Blasket sunshine.

Island Romance

One day merged into another as my stay on the Great Blasket Island entered its fourth week. The mainland and the events taking place there became irrelevant. My existence had gradually taken on the rhythm of island life. Daylight and darkness, sunshine and rain, determined the pace and process of my day. As the sun arced through the sky and the clouds floated across the sea, every angle offered a fresh perspective on the world. My days were suddenly bursting with life. Each moment pulsed with excitement. With the new dawn I breathed fresh energy.

Morning led me to the isolation at the far end of the island. Evening led me to the communal hearth in Sue's house. She and I exchanged reports on the seals, the dolphin, the chough family, the falcons, the tides, the weather and the sunset.

One evening, a teenage girl sat at Sue's fireside. I had seen her a few times as I returned home at the end of the day. She came into the island every day on the ferry and sat for hours reading on a fish box outside the remains of *Teach an Rí*. Although it was the dwelling closest to mine, I always succeeded in passing her by with just the briefest nod. Sue introduced us as I stood in the doorway. Had I been left to my own devices, it would have taken me a long time before I introduced myself to her. Her name was Aisling. She was sixteen and the granddaughter of a Blasket Islander. She was also a native Irish speaker. Her sister had started a small book business, and Aisling was the one charged with the task of selling them to the day-trippers on the Blasket. Aisling loved the island. Every day was an adventure. Irrespective of whether she made sales or did not make sales, her day was full and exciting.

From the day of our meeting onwards, I served her a cup of tea on her fish box as she set up shop in the mornings. She worked her way through her book supplies, reading both the Irish and English versions of each title during that summer. Sometimes she translated passages of island folklore for me, providing the seeds for the daydreams of my rambles.

One day, I returned from my walk at lunchtime to escape the blazing sun. The island was swarming with tourists. Squeals and shouts carried on the breeze from the direction of the beach. A steady stream of visitors struggled up the path past my door. Two large American men towered over Aisling outside *Teach an Rí*. 'You are a real Irish colleen. Gee, she's got the cutest freckles and green eyes.'

'My great-granddaddy came from Ireland. Ma-hoe-ney, from Cork. My wife's maternal grandmother was a MacIntyre from County Monaghan. Now, her first cousin was born in Leitrim and . . .' When I emerged from the hut twenty minutes later, Aisling was still smiling bravely up into the face from which the monologue streamed. Her face and neck were burned red. She attempted to deal with other potential customers and escape into the shade of *Teach an Rí*, but the man did not appear to draw even a breath.

I stood at my door and called down to her. 'Aisling dear, come up for your lunch now.'

She looked up at me in surprise as the man launched into another lecture about the lineage of his second cousins on his father's side. 'Don't you be delaying those nice gentlemen now, and get up here for your lunch.'

'Coming, Mam,' she called. 'I'm sorry. I have to go. Did you want to buy anything?' As he began a lengthy explanation as to why he was unable to buy anything, Aisling scampered up the bank and raced into my hut. I closed the door and we watched through the crack until the coast was clear. The men passed by slowly, presumably speculating as to how any family could live in a 3 metre by 1.5 metre cowshed. 'You should have told me to call my ten brothers and sisters as well,' Aisling giggled.

My provisions had reduced to porridge, rice, tea, tinned fish and beans, none of which tempted my newly acquired daughter. She explained that she normally went over to the cafe for chocolate and Coke but she just had not had a chance. A crowd of visitors still bustled around her little shop. Rather than dealing with them, I opted to go to the cafe for her.

So I headed off nervously, up past the *Dáil* and across to the cafe to make my first island purchase. I stepped in my bare feet over the rough ground outside the hostel. Both doors were open. Inside one door, a woman sat writing at a table. Inside the other, some walkers were cooking. Beyond this was the cafe where a dark-haired girl was handing out drinks over a half-door to heat-weary day-trippers. I approached and gave Aisling's order. 'Two Mars Bars and a can of Diet Coke, please.'

'There can't be two people on the island with that lunch order. That has to be for Aisling.' I nodded. 'You must be the girl staying in Ray's? There are rumours that you exist. Now I have proof.' While she chatted, she proceeded to make a tuna sandwich. 'She'll eat tuna, that's about all. I don't know how she manages to have such beautiful skin, what with all the chocolate she eats.' Between serving other customers, making sandwiches and baking, she continued to chat. Finally she leaned on the half-door again and introduced herself. Her name was Laura and she was from Canada. Her father was Russian. She had worked with a touring dramatic group on the European circuit and now was doing her own little tour. The European tour had become the Blasket stopover. She just could not leave the place. Every day she walked the island before the ferries arrived and then again after they left. Her routine was the reverse of mine. Working in the cafe earned her enough to survive. 'Now, I know someone who would like to deliver a take-away tuna sandwich.' With that, I was relieved of my messenger duty. A sixteen-year-old boy who worked in the cafe jumped at the task entrusted to him with obvious enthusiasm. Laura leaned on the door, gazing dreamily after him. 'Young love. Romance begins on the Great Blasket. Well, for some of us. We won't see him for an hour.' She had slipped a second can of Coke into the bag. Each time there was a lull in customer orders, she picked up a wind mobile she was making and threaded extra shells and feathers onto it. 'Men! Wouldn't you easily know one man owns the place and another runs it? There's not a picture, an ornament or a mirror in the place.' Laura's stamp could be seen already here and there. On the deep windowsills sat two dramatic pieces of driftwood. 'Nothing – neither a map of the island, nor a photo of Peig on the wall. It was her house after all.' She seemed to be able to do ten things at once, all the while chatting with me and laughing with the dozens of tourists. Every so often she took a glance out over the half-door, down to the left. Some distance away, a TV reporter was interviewing a man. 'We'll have to wait to hear the great plans on the telly.'

After a few minutes Seán came hurrying up the bank to the cafe. 'Everything under control?' He needn't have asked. Laura could run the place single-handedly while blindfolded. 'Where's Colm?'

Laura looked up, feigning surprise. 'Oh, has he gone out?'

I was about to disappear when the cameraman hailed me. 'Can you lean on the door, as you were a few minutes ago, and the two of you continue talking?' I excused myself and suggested that he shoot the many other tourists around instead. 'No. The frayed shirt looks great against the backdrop of the cottage.'

'You mean the brown legs look great,' Laura challenged him from inside. The cameraman's colleague, a reporter, immediately intervened, as I turned away, embarrassed.

'We just want a shot of the heads chatting over the door,' he assured me.

'Come on,' Laura said to me. 'My mom will see me on TV at last. Will you broadcast this in Canada? I can call my mom.' The cameraman took her seriously and began to explain that *Nationwide* was broadcast on RTÉ, only in Ireland.

I leaned on the door, as directed, and held a most self-conscious conversation with Laura. As I left, she called after me. 'Drop up to the hostel some evening.'

I walked back along the rabbit track. A cluster of students were peering in the window of my hut when I returned, so I sat on a grassy mound outside the *Dáil* and waited. When the coast was clear, I ducked inside and put water on the stove to make some tea. Then, armed with two steaming mugs, I dropped down to Aisling and suggested to her admirer that he'd better get back to work and have an alibi at the ready for Seán when he arrived at the cafe. He looked at his watch in shock and sped off.

'Colm teaches sailing in Dingle and he crewed on a huge

sailing ship in the Tall Ships race. He saw whales and millions of dolphins and . . .' Aisling was as smitten as her admirer. We decided that, from now on, she had to close up shop and get to the cafe for lunch, even if business was brisk. There were more important things in life than making money, such as an island romance.

'Anita, there's somebody after opening your door and going into your house,' said Aisling. I looked up in surprise. A troop of about twenty boys were gathered around my door. I raced up and squeezed my way through. A female youth leader stood at my bed, reading my journal.

'Excuse me, this is a private house. Do you mind?'

'Told ya, Miss,' came a voice from outside. But the woman was not going to be shown up by a child.

'Nothing is private on this island. It's owned by the state.'

How the state could claim ownership of my diary was a mystery to me. I took the journal from her. 'Actually, the island is privately owned. The state lost its claim on the island in the courts,' I said as I stood by the door, holding it open, 'Do you mind?'

She brushed past me without as much as a sideways glance in my direction.

'There's not much to see in there anyway. Follow me,' she barked. The young boys marched after her on the double.

'I can't believe her rudeness.' Aisling was standing below my door ready to lend moral support.

I spent the remainder of the evening in the anonymity of the crowd of tourists on the beach. Gradually, the crowd thinned out and after the last ferry departed, I ventured back up through the deserted village to the cowshed. Peace had been restored once more.

In the distance, Sue waved to me from where she stood beside her clothes line. Two rabbits were nibbling an apple core beside the well. Aisling's box leaned against the gable of *Teach an Rí*. I wondered if she had got the same ferry as Colm back across to the mainland. I would just have to wait until the following day to find out how the romance was progressing. At my door, I found she had left a book of folklore for me on the step. I noticed Seán climb the hill up to An Gob. He stopped occasionally to gaze out to sea. On the beach, Laura stood in the shallow waves watching the Beverley Sisters. Then two ewes wandered past me, reclaiming their ground. I looked at them chomping on the short grass and occasional nettle. I sat on the bank, in the sunshine with Aisling's book and felt thoroughly at home. It was then that I began to feel part of the tiny island community.

The Blasket village in sunshine.

The Screaming Womb

Of all the Blasket folklore, the romance of Eileen and Tomás is certainly worth telling. It was said to be the perfect match. Eileen was lively and fun-loving, with a singing voice to make a skylark blush. Tomás was strong and hardworking, blessed with the skill of a master fiddler. Both families were delighted with the arrangement.

Each evening, for several months, Eileen and her mother, Norah, sewed her wedding dress. This, with its fine lace bodice created from her grandmother's beautiful shawl, would rival any made in Dingle. Her godmother, Céit, in Springfield, Massachusetts, sent a new gleaming white veil with hundreds of tiny white rose blossoms interlacing the threads. Eileen packed and repacked her trousseau every day.

'Asthore, you'd be thinking it was off to America you were going instead of down into the Lower Village. Can't you come back up if something do be forgotten?' her father teased.

Laughing, Eileen would continue with her checking and packing. After all, she was heading off to her own New World, where she would have her house, husband and children, with all the responsibilities and possibilities that entailed.

Tomás was kept busy too. He went fishing with his father and his brother, Páid, making the most of the good weather.

In bad weather, Páid laboured with him, hauling stones to build a two-room dwelling for Tomás and Eileen.

The weeks raced by. The June sun brought the sea birds into the islands where the boys of the village braved the steepness of the cliffs in search of prized eggs. Tomás joined expeditions across to An Téaracht to hunt puffins. The seals moved off the Blasket Island, leaving the strand smooth and sparkling. Men talked over banks and walls, unfurling their backs after a winter of bracing winds and violent storms. Women stood and chatted at the well, marvelling at the speed with which Tomás was finishing off the roof of his house and delighting in the growing belly of Páid's wife, Máire, who was expecting their first child at the end of the lobster season. They debated whether or not her bump was lying to the back; if it was, the older women decreed that it would be a boy. And everyone talked of the wedding of Tomás and Eileen, planned for the end of the month.

The third Saturday in June dawned a warm cloudless day. The waters of the Blasket Sound were a sparkling turquoise. Beiginis glistened under a veil of summer dew. The islanders were up early, donning their Sunday best. At eight o'clock, it was time to depart for the wedding ceremony on the mainland. Tomás had left earlier with his family. As Eileen strode down the path to the harbour, the older women and young children followed, chattering and fussing. Norah stowed her daughter's trousseau carefully in a wooden trunk for the crossing. Eileen would dress in her cousin's house on the mainland, where a bouquet of yellow roses from her aunt's prized bush awaited her. As the last of the sleek black *naomhógs* glided effortlessly out into the blue water of the Blasket Sound, the cheers of the old and very young remaining in on the island faded in their wake.

It was said that Eileen and Tomás were the handsomest

couple ever to walk down the aisle of the church in Ballyferriter. They received presents from friends and family on the Blasket, the mainland and even some from America. The island celebrations lasted for two days and after that Tomás and Eileen lit a fire in their new hearth on the Blasket Island, and their married life began.

Eileen's first year was spent in a flurry of excitement, settling into her own home. In all weathers, she worked in the North Field, side by side with her husband. While Tomás and Páid went fishing, Eileen and her sister-in-law, Máire, became very close friends. Many happy days Eileen spent looking after Máire's baby while Máire and their mother-in-law worked in the field or gathered seaweed at low tide. Eileen sang and took a secret delight in the baby, who nuzzled into her breast for comfort and often sucked her blouse hungrily. When the women returned to the house, they always said the same thing: 'Sure it won't be long at all before you're suckling one of your own.' Each time Eileen heard this, her heart jumped in anticipation, wondering when she and Tomás would be blessed with a child, but God did not choose to bless them in the first two years of married life.

As the seals returned, and the wheatears' song disappeared for a third winter, Máire became pregnant with her second child. Eileen nearly burst with excitement for her sister-in-law as the news was whispered to her over the garden wall one bright November morning. She smiled and hugged Máire, but some part of her soul sank with the yearning and emptiness in her own heart. Yet, for the next six months, Eileen was an enthusiastic support and help to her friend. Little baby Niamh was born the following June, on the fourth wedding anniversary of Eileen and Tomás. They were chosen as godparents to the child. As Eileen cuddled and breathed the scented softness of her godchild's skin, the impatience and ache cried within her. Her own mother's constant reassurance – 'All in God's good time' – failed to deliver the soothing balm of earlier years.

After five years, the empty cradle, a wedding present from her aunt, stood neglected behind some lobster pots in the shed. Although banished from the house they heard it cry through every sigh within their walls. A silence settled like a cloud over their home as Tomás and Eileen stopped singing and playing music together. For a time they rode the waves of normality despite the ominous undercurrent. Neither ever mentioned their grief, as if it was some secret to be shielded from the other. Then Tomás began to spend more time fishing, hunting and visiting other houses at night. Eileen found herself alone working in the house, labouring in the field and waiting at night. She began to dread the loneliness of the dark winter evenings. Soon she began to fear the arrival of Tomás at night. Her husband's anger intensified towards her. She kept the best table and the best house in the village, yet he would find fault: she oversalted the fish; she talked too much; she never salted the fish; she never talked to him. The hope that had lured her from month to month had long since been quenched. Her mother said she must be patient and all would be well 'in God's good time'.

One evening as she waited for Tomás, she wondered if God had forgotten about her. Her husband's supper lay cold and untouched on the table. The candles had burned out hours before. She sat by the hearth staring at the embers. Tears didn't come any more. Maybe she had cried them all. The ticking of the clock became a rhythm from another world. The roaring of the waves on the White Strand lulled her into a comforting stillness. She slipped deeper into its soft darkness and silence.

The fire died and the room grew cold as Eileen slept.

Just before 3 a.m. the latch lifted and the door swung violently open, crashing against the side of the dresser. The crockery rattled and a jug smashed on the floor. Eileen gasped with fright, struggling between worlds. Tomás stumbled towards the hearth. 'You can't even keep the fire lighting,' he snarled at her. Her heart thundered as she opened her eyes, disorientated. Vaguely, she was aware of Tomás' silhouette swaying before the hearth. Suddenly, everything turned red, as a blow struck the side of her face. 'You can't even do that right, can you?' Her brain jolted against the side of her skull, sending a fantail of lightning flashes swirling across her vision. She held her head in an effort to stop it spinning. She felt tingling as her jaw began to swell. She thought that she had spoken, begging to know what she had done wrong. Then she realised that no words had come out. She felt her mouth in the darkness. It throbbed and felt sticky and wet.

Tomás steadied himself against the settle and spat into the hearth. 'You can do nothing right, can you? You can't even give me a child.' Her heart lunged so violently against her throat, she could not breathe. 'Can't even give me a child.' The words echoed through the room. They grew louder and louder, until they seemed to echo through the whole village. The waves took up the mantra and beat it onto the rocks, over and over. The caves breathed it into the darkness until it resounded faster. She saw *An Fear Marbh* heave his bulk from the sea and roar to the sky. 'Can't even give me a child.' Then Eileen saw no more as the noise drowned her consciousness.

The next day the word spread from woman to woman at the well. 'Isn't she a terror, the way she do let the fire out, and then can't see in the darkness?'

'Lord save us, but didn't she give herself a terrible fall entirely?'

'Didn't she strike her head on the corner of the table as she went down?'

'Tomás hasn't left her bedside at all. Sure he's worried to death about her.'

'Did you know it was three days before she did come back to herself?'

'Isn't she blessed with the kind, patient man she do have?'

Norah kept house for her daughter through her illness. She never pried, but her presence eased Eileen back from her fright, until the dam burst and her tears flooded forth. Finally, through sobs, the words came: 'Tomás says I can't give him a child. I can't even do that.'

'And how is Tomás so sure that he has the child to give, alanna?'

Eileen stared in amazement at her mother. Never did it occur to her that anyone but she could be at fault. For a long time, she had begun to believe her husband: that she could do nothing right. She could neither cook nor sew. She could neither tend a fire nor conceive a child.

'What did your grandmother tell you about putting blame on other people?' Eileen pointed her finger and looked down at it. She remembered the words so well.

'Every time you do point an accusing finger at someone, you do be pointing three at yourself,' she answered, as she looked at the three fingers pointing back at herself. 'So maybe Tomás is afraid that it is *he* who can't father a child for me.'

'Maybe he is, Eileen, and maybe he's afraid and angry with himself, and not with you. Sometimes, it's harder for men to accept these things. Whatever it is, with the help of God, we'll find a way.'

From that day out, Eileen and Norah set to work. Eileen told Tomás that she knew it was time that she found a cure for their sorrow. They had never given it words before, except for the night that Tomás had struck her. Men and women did not talk about these things; they just happened. Tomás looked at her, confused. Her new composure and confidence took him by surprise. As he spoke, he reverted his gaze to his mug of tea.

'Well, you women do know more about these things. I'll leave it to you to solve your problem.' He never looked up, just continued with his food. For the three days of each of the next five full moons, Eileen and Norah collected green herbs and roots. Eileen boiled them for three hours. At sunset, she cooled the infusion. She strained a full bowl of the brown liquid, added three drops of holy water and drank the full amount before she lay with her husband.

Tomás seemed to have faith in the knowledge of the women. He relaxed and resembled the Tomás of old in many ways. After five months of herbal infusions, Eileen felt ill but not from pregnancy. It was time to visit Nell, the island healer. Norah visited her alone first, saying, 'It wouldn't do to have the whole village discussing your sorrow.'

The following morning, after Tomás set off fishing with Páid, Norah came through the door. 'Nell tells me that Tomás was very sick as a teenager, with mumps.' Eileen stood by the door with Norah, watching the *naomhóg* slice through the rolling sea. Eileen did not understand the significance of what she was being told, until her mother explained that mumps could lead to impotence in a young man. Now she understood that it probably was not her fault.

'Tomás is the man you want as your husband.' Eileen looked at her mother puzzled. She was not sure if this was a statement or a question.

'Of course,' she answered finally.

'But you want a child?'

'More than anything in the world, Mam. We both want a child.'

It was then that Norah took Eileen up to see the old healer, Nell, who explained about the cure on the mainland. Nell told her that it was the only way to conceive a child, and keep her husband.

Word was quick to spread from the well.

'Isn't it great for Nell, going across for to see her sister on the mainland?'

'It is, and she the great age that she is. Sure, it is only that Eileen and Norah agreed for to take the old woman that she can go at all.'

'And what do an old woman like her want to make that trip for? 'Tis at home saying her prayers she should be.'

There was always one with the bitter word.

'Isn't her old widowed sister sick and maybe dying. Would you be begrudging her a last visit?'

There were nods all round, and that was an end to it. The women sent their prayers with Nell for her sick sister, and they praised Eileen and Norah for giving up their time to look after a cranky old woman on such a trip.

Meanwhile, Nell explained to Tomás the importance of the plants growing on the mainland. In on the island, there wasn't the variety. The island herbs that she had tried had not worked for Eileen. It was vital that certain plants on the mainland were picked and prepared during the full moon. As Tomás knew, it was then that the sap was at its richest and most potent. The herbs had to be picked and consumed within the same moonlight. Eileen and Norah would stay with Nell in her sister's house. He need have no worries about his wife. Tomás was grateful to the old woman; he firmly believed her story of the herbal cure on the mainland for Eileen.

The three women set off in the *naomhóg* with Tomás and Páid. The tide was high because of the full moon. Eileen sat breathless in the bow of the boat, her body glowing with anticipation and anxiety. Tomás noted his wife's flushed face, and prayed to God to find her a cure this time and end his shame. Eileen gripped her bag nervously, avoiding his gaze. She watched the cliffs of Dún Chaoin rising before her, as she had done on the morning of her wedding five years before.

As the two older women made slow progress up the slipway at Dún Chaoin, Eileen turned to wave at the small black *naomhóg*. Páid's voice carried over the water. 'Don't you be drinking too much porter with your sister, Nell. We don't want you falling into the waves on the way back.' Eileen sat down on the coffin step halfway up the slipway.

'Tomás thinks I've come out here for a cure,' she sobbed, covering her face in shame.

'It is a cure of a kind you've come out for, alanna,' Nell gasped as she reached the coffin step.

'Don't you want to keep your husband and have a baby?' her mother asked her.

'You know I do, Mam.'

'Well then, let's go, for it's a long walk to the church.'

The three women linked arms and set off slowly, leaving the sea and Nell's sister's house far behind.

Three days later, as they stood on the clifftop, looking across into the island for the first sign of the boat, Nell quickly gathered a bunch of herbs and pressed them into Eileen's hand. 'Make sure he sees you boiling these tonight. Give him half the tea to drink and you drink the other half. And don't forget you must lie with him within the week. You'll both be very happy. God works in mysterious ways.' With that she set off, hobbling down the slipway. Norah gave her daughter's hand a reassuring squeeze and they followed.

The following month Eileen knew she was with child. Her breasts ached, and she felt a warm glow throughout her body. She sang from morning till night, treasuring her happiness privately until the time was right to tell her husband. Tomás came into the house to take a burning ember from the fire to patch the *naomhóg*. 'Put that back,' she scolded happily. 'No ember can leave this house until the things that are inside are out.' Tomás knew the significance of the superstition better than anyone. He dropped the tongs in shock. He kissed her, holding her as if she were a fragile china cup. Before the first woman had reached the well that Sunday morning, he had spread the news to every house on the island. As he set off to mass on the mainland, he was the proudest man on the Great Blasket Island.

When he returned from mass, he bounded up the cliff from the pier like a new lamb. He presented Eileen with a holy medal of the Virgin and Child, wrapped in soft white paper. 'Father Muiris blessed this for you and the baby, when he heard our good news. He asked me to be sure to give it to you.'

Eileen felt the flush surge from the base of her neck. She took the medal and stared at Our Lady and the Infant Jesus in her arms. She could not speak. It was Tomás, not she, who added, 'He's a grand man. Sure if it's a boy, can't we call the baby Muiris after him?'

Eight months later, Eileen had a fine healthy son. He was baptised by and named after Father Muiris, the priest in the church in Ballyferriter. The womenfolk said that the baby would be twice blessed for it.

Russian Requiem

Routine began to restore the security and predictability that had been stolen from my life for so long. I regained control and felt free. During the month of August, I found and followed my own daily schedule. I swam first thing in the morning under the watchful eye of the Beverley Sisters, then had breakfast, filled my water bottle, collected a scone and jam from Laura at the cafe, and set off on my adventure to the back of the island.

That day, I followed the cliffs over past the beach and continued to the Gravel Strand. Sitting on the clifftop, I watched the familiar grey seals hauled out on two small islands of rock, Carraig Fhada and Oileán Buí. Daydreams and stories were far from my mind. My thoughts were in the cold darkness beneath the waves. I had heard the news of the *Kursk*, a Russian nuclear submarine lost miles beneath the freezing Barents Sea in the Arctic, with the trapped crew believed to be still alive. As one of the seals slid in off the rocks and submerged, I wondered what it saw in the deep waters off the Great Blasket Island. The *Quebra*, a First World War munitions ship, was down there somewhere. Perhaps the seal would swim over the cargo of wire and artillery shells scattered in the gullies, 15 to 27 metres below, her shadow gliding between the huge boilers that still stand upright on the wreck. An army diver had told me that the wreck was intact, the hull was very sound and a recoil spring from one of the ship's guns was still visible, owing to the protection of the cliffs. I imagined that the seal would ignore that, being more interested in the shoals of fish feeding around the wreck. My thoughts returned to the *Kursk* crew and I shivered in the sunshine, as I thought of the freezing temperatures and silent darkness that the lost men would be experiencing. Closing my eyes, I willed through every atom of my being for them to be rescued and hauled back up to the sunshine.

After some time, I stirred myself and continued on my way, following the jagged cut in the cliff towards the Seal Cove. As I drew closer, my pace quickened in anticipation. Each morning, I loved to check in on the island's only baby seal, and see how he was getting on. I lay down on my stomach with my head peering over the steep cliff. Sixty or seventy metres below me, the inlet was strewn with what looked like large rounded boulders. I watched intently, waiting for one to move and clap its fins together. As I waited, kittiwakes rose before my eyes on updrafts of air, filling the sky with their cries. Suddenly, what I had thought to be a round white boulder caught my eye as it rolled over and stretched its neck towards a stem of oarweed. Through the binoculars, I could see his antics clearly. As he tugged at the air, missing his target every time, one of his flippers swam frantically like a clockwork toy, in a vain attempt to propel himself forward. He had moved a good ten metres down the beach since the previous morning. I wondered how he had done it. Each time, his mother came in to nurse him, she nudged and pushed him back up to the cliff. It was a laborious exercise, but vital for his survival, as this little ball of pure white fur could not swim yet. It would take a full three weeks of suckling his mother before he would have enough blubber to survive in the sea, and he was not even two weeks old. Junior was oblivious to the incoming tide, and with every stretch for the weed, he inched farther down the beach.

'Get back up there where your mother left you,' I roared, not thinking that he would hear my voice over the thundering of the waves, but he did. He stopped his quest suddenly, lifting his head towards me. Through the binoculars, I could see his two huge black eyes staring in my direction. The incoming tide was only a metre or so from him. I scanned the rollers beyond the bay entrance, but there was no sign of his mother. I knew he would not survive if he were swept out to sea. I barked at him as loudly as I could. He responded by barking and rolling onto his back where he clapped his flippers together, as I had seen him do every time he was enjoying himself playing or suckling. As we continued this banter, I wondered if my babysitting game would distract him from his progress towards the water until his mother returned or the tide turned. So far it was working. Gradually, instead of making towards the sea, he was stretching parallel to the tide in my direction. I stood up slowly, keeping my head in view over the clifftop as I walked away from the sea. Every few metres I stopped and we re-established contact. After an hour and a half, I was hoarse and exhausted, but the seal pup was at least three metres back up from the sea.

I had just resolved to sacrifice my walk for the day in order to keep an eye on Junior, when I was relieved of my babysitting duties. The huge cow hauled herself out onto the beach, trailing a dark, glistening path in her wake as she slid over the hot stones. The pup was yelping and shaking in anticipation as she came close to him. He began pucking her belly excitedly, searching out her teats, but she was having none of it. Unceremoniously, she rolled and jostled the pup in front of her, until he was well up beyond the high-tide line. Below me, under the shelter of the cliff, she began to nurse the pup. Beyond the surf, the distinctive big head of a bull seal kept watch over the mother and wayward child. On the beach, the earlier playground of the pup was now submerged, and the single stem of seaweed had been swept away. Relieved to hand the responsibility back to Mother, I set off up to the fort.

That afternoon, while returning along the south road, I heard the distinctive blow of a whale east of An Gob. I sat back against a dagger-like rock that pierced the side of the cliff and scanned the undulating waters that sparkled over 150 metres below. It was the time of year for whales to migrate along the 100-metre contour west of Inis Tuaisceart, travelling to and from warmer breeding waters. I had seen one close to Inis Mhic Uibhleain the previous week but never this close. I knew that they could stay submerged for over an hour but if it was a large school of whales, the chances of seeing something as these colossal creatures cruised majestically by was much greater, so I waited.

Suddenly I heard a great explosion as a waterspout sprayed high into the air. The huge rounded black back arched through the surface as the whale submerged. The tail flukes flicked and slapped the water as it disappeared. I jumped up in excitement. Close by, another spout exploded, followed closely by two more. A school of whales *was* cruising by! At the height I stood above them, it was impossible to gauge their size. They frolicked and displayed, as if they knew they were in protected Irish waters.

Suddenly, a whale rose vertically into the blue sky. For a second, it seemed to be suspended in the air, before it slapped onto its back with a spectacular, explosive crash. Then another broke out into the sunshine and returned in a white blossom of spray. In turn, each great water creature threw itself against the sun, fusing sky and sea in a flash of sparks. The electricity pulsated through my body. As each broke the surface and blew, a shout leaped from my chest. Each launch melted the heavens and the ocean into one. Thousands of birds wheeled around the dancing sea creatures. The sea opened and closed to the sky, as the surface bubbled with life. Breathless, I watched and watched, hardly daring to blink, until their trail faded from view in the sea to the south.

When they had disappeared, I flopped back down against the rock, light-headed and laughing, my body vibrating with the energy of sun and sea. I watched the veil of sea birds that had shadowed the whales turn in unison and return to the island. Their noise rose to a deafening pitch, as the keening of thousands of birds suddenly echoed against the cliffs. The island tolled with the sound, and I became aware in their cries of the requiem song for 118 young Russian men.

The whales had now disappeared without trace. The defining lines of sea and sky returned as if nothing had happened, but I knew that it had. I stood for a long time, the sole witness of their passing, with a cold emptiness in my stomach. It was after sunset before I turned away from the silent sea and returned home to the village.

Do or Die

The climb down to the Gravel Strand was unnerving. I made cautious progress, weighing the pros and cons of each step and handhold as I descended. Sigrid swam in the cove frequently and so clambered down sure-footed as a goat. Since this German woman kept to herself as much as I did, it had been quite some time before we had made one another's acquaintance on the Great Blasket Island. When she met me for the first time, I was in the middle of one of my daily conversations with the seal pup. That seemed to break the ice between us easily. Neither she nor I was the focus of the attention, as we doted over the cuddly ball of fur and mischief, and so a relaxed friendship developed.

Each summer, when the German kindergarten where Sigrid worked closed for the holidays, she escaped from the city and flew to Ireland. She camped on the Great Blasket Island for her six-week break, returning to Germany only two days before the school reopened.

In the stormy weather of that summer, her tent had ripped in two, and so she had moved into the hostel. Most days, she lay on the beach, becoming a darker shade of mahogany. Each time we met, we stopped and exchanged reports of the seal pup, the falcons, the very pregnant donkey or the sunset. Then, one day, Sigrid said she would take me swimming on the Gravel Strand, through the sea arch and into the seal caves. I was both excited and terrified at the prospect.

The low morning sun just brushed the clifftop, where my shoes and towel lay abandoned. Below, the cove was dark and steep-walled, with black water breathing in the shadows. The rise and fall was violent, making hollow, thudding sounds in under the cliffs. Sigrid was already a tiny blonde head bobbing on the black swell. With each breaststroke, she swam farther out from the gravel beach. I dropped onto the cold pebbles and crunched down to the water's edge. I followed her, gasping in the icy water and struggling to keep a central path between the cliffs, for fear of being scraped up and down the rock faces. As the water heaved, I was launched skyward like a helpless rag doll. Then, just as suddenly, the sea sank beneath me and I dropped as fast as a stone. Exhausted, I turned at the mouth of the bay and looked back into the gloom. As we trod water, Sigrid indicated the narrow sea arch on the left. For a few seconds, I saw it open, a silver window of light, until the swell rose and slapped it closed with a thunderous roar. I watched the rhythm of light and dark, all the while my heart racing faster.

The old battle for survival began in my head once more. You can stay as you are, tread water until you drown, or stand up to the terror and overcome it. At once, the arch became the focus of my life. Passing through it became the only way to escape. With my heart pounding in my throat, I swam slowly towards the arch. How many strokes? When to start? If I mistimed, I would crack my head open like an egg. Behind me, Sigrid was saying something that I could not understand. Then she was beside me. 'I swam through it yesterday, on low tide,' she said. 'It was great. Pity we can't do it today.' I pulled myself within reach, then reverse-kicked, to keep out of the suction.

I had to do it; I could see no other way. I imagined myself lunging forward on a count of ten, only to realise that I had not moved. Several times I counted and failed to move. I believed that if I did not succeed, I would not survive anything. The reasoning was dubious, but the outcome was realistic. If I didn't get through, I wouldn't be alive to attempt anything else. 'Don't get too close,' Sigrid shouted. Suddenly, on the count of ten, I shot forward. My arms glided through the dappled reflections. Almost at once, I felt the surge launch me up into the roof of the arch. I don't remember jack-knifing. I remember kicking desperately and dragging myself along the rock walls. My fingertips bled, and I felt a burning pain, as the roof of the sea arch skinned the backs of my legs. The water turned, surging back, blinding my face with my hair. I kicked against it with all my strength.

When I broke through the surface of the water, choking and gasping, I was still kicking for all I was worth. 'You're through, you're through, Anita. Stop!' Sigrid roared. I glanced around frantically, still fleeing for my life. She was right: I had got through. I stopped and struggled for air, until my breath came back. As we trod water closer to the shore, I became aware of the stinging of my hands and legs.

'That was close,' Sigrid said, shocked.

Farther along the cliff, the high tide still gave a good metre's clearance under the wide mouth of the seal cave. I swam slowly after Sigrid into the darkness, taking care to keep to the side this time. She had warned me never to block a seal's line of escape. At first, we could see nothing in the darkness. We rose with the swell and heard the heavy thud as the water slopped into the caverns and cracks in the cave, echoing, deep and resonant. Gradually I began to make out spear-like stalactites hanging from the dark roof and a pebbled shore against the back wall of the cave. The swell surged into it, crunching and flooding the gravel before draining and sucking noisily as it retreated once more. I held my arm outstretched against the wall, holding my position. The light bounced off the water surface under the cave mouth, before shattering into shards of dancing reflections on the cave roof. To the right of the gravel shore I could make out a few dark, rounded shapes. As we watched, one seal turned and was obviously looking in our direction. Before they took fright, we turned slowly and glided out on the next wave.

Back up at the hostel, Laura provided some dressing for my cuts. Then she listened eagerly to the next instalment of the adventures of the seal pup, as she served the last tourists of the day.

'Sigrid brought turf briquettes from the mainland yesterday, and I have a pile of driftwood, so it's dinner and a fire tonight,' she announced. 'Come up after sunset, and bring any extra candles you have. You know how thrifty Seán is with candles; he thinks we're all owls.' I had heard that Seán was worried about fire in the hostel and naturally he did not want candles burning, yet the few hostel lanterns had a habit of walking. As a result, Laura ended up operating in darkness. I promised candles and departed, relishing the thought of a proper dinner later at Peig's fireside.

As the sun disappeared to the west of Inis Tuaisceart, I set off across the rabbit path to Peig's house. The air was still and expectant. Seán had said that there would be thunder. I arrived at the half-door as the first heavy raindrops began to fall. I lifted the latch to Laura's greeting, 'And the Lord said "Let there be light", and about time too.' Inside, Sigrid and Laura's faces glowed in the firelight. The shadow of a giant chair quivered on the far wall, while above it Laura tossed the metre-high shadow of her head. 'Now, at last, we can *see* our dinner,' she said as she helped me light my two candles and four small tea lights. Sigrid balanced a tray covered in aluminium foil behind the candles, and the reflection was thrown across the room.

I pulled up a chair to the fire. 'No wonder Seán is worried about fire,' I laughed, looking at the great branch of driftwood that rested on the flagstones, at the far end consumed in the flames. As it turned from orange to black and burned to ashes, Laura nudged it farther into the hearth with her foot. 'Well, I suppose Peig did the same and she had no trouble,' I said.

'No trouble! The woman had a miserable life. No, correction: she *was* a misery,' Laura admonished. 'Have you read that godawful book of hers?'

'I have, at secondary school. Every student in Ireland had to read it. *Peig* was on the Irish language syllabus for years.'

'How did students handle it?'

Suddenly I had flashbacks of pages of vocabulary, translated painstakingly from *Peig* into my copybook, and the dire panic before exams.

'We hated it' was my understatement.

'But surely *The Islandman* or *Twenty Years a-Growing* would have been more suitable for teenagers?'

I had to agree with Sigrid. *An t-Oileánach* by Tomás Ó Criomhthain and *Fiche Bliain ag Fás* by Muiris Ó Súilleabháin brought island people to life again. As a teenager, after a visit to the Great Blasket Island, I had devoured the two books. Of all the visitors that I had encountered since my arrival, there were always more hunting for Tomás Ó Criomhthain's and Muiris Ó Súilleabháin's houses than for Peig's.

'Well, before we start bad-mouthing Peig in her own house, remember that her stories were modified dramatically before publication,' I hastened to point out.

'That's terrible. Why didn't they publish what she said?' Laura was irate.

'Well, apparently, she was fairly feisty and outspoken. She wrote about a lot of things, and spoke in a way that may have given offence to the Irish Catholic masses of the early 1930s. Church and state were one and the same, so I suppose anything on the state exam syllabus was bound to be sterilised and sanitised before it was read by the pure, impressionable youth of Ireland.'

'Well, Peig, there will be no censorship in your house tonight. To Peig!' With that, Laura raised her glass to the woman of the house.

Sigrid and I echoed the toast. Laura spooned out the curry in front of the fire and we started dinner. Occasionally, a puff of smoke was blown back down the chimney. Outside, the rain splashed noisily from the gutter, turning the path into mud in the darkness. Inside, the conversation and laughter got louder while Peig's kitchen got warmer.

'If you think meeting a seal cow is dangerous, you should try meeting a bear.'

'A bear?' Sigrid was eyeing Laura sceptically. 'And who has met a Mammy Bear? Do tell us.'

'Who do you think?' I asked, still laughing after Laura's last story.

'For absent company,' Laura said, as she poured a glass of wine for Peig, which was placed ceremoniously on the mantle. I wondered if any of the few island emigrants who returned from the New World told stories to match Laura's. Having poured Peig's drink, she launched into yet another.

'Before I started travelling in Europe, I spent two years working in grizzly bear country. The job was advertised in college. Plant trees in a beautiful, mountainous wilderness and *get paid* for it. It seemed idyllic. I was going to save the planet.

I had signed up and was on my induction course before I knew what I was letting myself in for. I was going to plant trees in the Canadian wilderness. We would be flown to some outback town, like Fort St John, from where we would be dropped by helicopter to our planting zone. They drop you off with a couple of hundred boxes of saplings, a backpack and a foreman who is armed with a rifle and a radio. That's it for two whole weeks. Well, they always said two weeks, but we never saw the chopper before the month was out. I arrived for the induction course, armed to the teeth with mosquito repellent, refreshing hand-wipes and every kind of deodorant spray imaginable. Our tutor's bear course was short and sweet: "Bears will smell you ten miles off, as you are now. You have to smell like the forest and the animals around you. No deodorants, shampoos, hand cream, body lotion, toothpaste or insect repellents. No cosmetics of any kind. (The last working group in zone B12 didn't take it seriously and so they had a fatality.) Don't hide in a tree. Black bears climb them and grizzly bears knock them. Be on your guard at all times. Women, if you've got your menstrual cycle, remember, you're a red rag to a bull!"

'As he spoke, I was counting the days of my cycle, anxiously. I was due to have my period during the first week of planting. I was going to die! I asked him what one should do in the event of one's menstrual cycle.

'..."Stay upwind of bears. Never plant alone. Always plant in twos or threes. Bears will attack a lone, weaker animal." (He kept looking at me.) "When you're being chased . . ." (I would have preferred "If". I began to have severe reservations about my chosen career path.) ". . . always run downhill, never uphill. Bears are slower and more awkward when going downhill. And don't forget: never climb a tree."

'Then he gave each one of us a whistle, making us hang them around our necks. "Blow this, if you're lost or being attacked. The noise might scare off the bear. If not, you make yourself look as big as you possibly can. Stretch up. Jump. Roar. Make noise. Let the bear think that you're as big as him, and therefore not worth the trouble."

'I began to pray that if I met a bear I would meet a blind one, or else I would need to grow pretty fast. So we were told to pack. I proceeded to *unpack* most of the things that I had packed at home. It was hardly worth the bother of taking the bag at all when I was finished. I had my last shower for at least a month. Like the others, I used no shampoos, lotions or deodorant. By the time we were choppered out to our planting zone, I can tell you, we were rancid.

'My worst fears came true. We were dumped in zone B12. When the noise of the chopper fades, it's the weirdest feeling. You're standing there, dwarfed by giant trees and mountain peaks as far as the eye can see – not another human being for a thousand miles. It's awesome. Then they strike.'

'The bears?' Sigrid was anticipating an attack.

'No, the bugs. Millions of bugs. They are everywhere: on your skin, under your skin, in your hair, your clothes, your food. You can't escape them. After two weeks, they stopped biting me, I probably smelt too bad but one of the guys nearly lost his mind. There wasn't a millimetre of his flesh that wasn't infected and swollen. He tore at his face until most of it bled. The noise of the bugs never stops, night or day. When one lot finish their shift, the new guys take over. We were so busy dealing with the bugs, we sort of forgot about the bears.

'When we arrived, the foreman divided out the boxes, and we set off into the forest. I dug a hole for each little sapling, broke up and softened the soil and then gently tucked in the roots. I talked encouragingly to every single one that I planted and sang to them. Stop smirking! It's scientifically proven that plants respond accordingly to a positive or negative sound. It's amazing how involved you become. I suppose I was feeling quite evangelical about it at the start. Each little sapling would grow and replace the great trees being massacred in the rainforests. Then, after a while, you become absorbed in the rhythm of planting. You lose yourself. It's a bit like meditation. Then a blister or a pain in your back brings you back into yourself. You look up and realise that you've been in another world for two hours. It's like being on this island: you shed all the distractions that you carry round on the mainland.

'There was one guy who didn't speak to anyone for a whole month; I don't know what was going on for him. Maybe it was the only way he could deal with it. Some people are not suited to it, but it's just tough luck if you discover that on Day One. You ain't going anywhere for two weeks.

'In the evening, you return to camp with your planting buddy and cook dinner. Then the foreman does the count of the boxes. The exact number that you planted during the day is meticulously recorded. Typically, in our group, the guys had a competition going. Who was going to earn the most money? I couldn't believe it – on the first night, one guy had eight boxes planted, another seven and another five. I hadn't stopped planting once and I was still under one box. I was so embarrassed, but not for long, when I discovered how they managed to get such figures. They just *shoved* the trees into the ground. Sometimes, they broke the roots, at other times the tree fell over as soon as it was planted. Most trees just dried out in the sun. In any case, most of them were dead by the end of the week and there was I, watering mine into the ground and checking them after a few days. I was so angry that I brought it up at the evening meeting. The guys laughed at me. So did the foreman. He was paid to count the numbers of trees missing from the boxes at night. It wasn't his job to see *how* we planted the trees, he said; that was up to us. I couldn't deal with this attitude. You could just tip the trees out and read a book for the day for all he cared. Anyway, after a few weeks, I came to accept that I couldn't be responsible for others or I would go off my trolley trying. So I continued gardening my saplings into the earth: at eighty cents a tree, I wouldn't become a millionaire, but at least I could live with myself.

'The first ten days were the hardest. My wrists, ankles, face and neck were covered in red lumps from mosquitoes and ants, and my hands were destroyed with blisters. It was tough going: some of the terrain was so rough and hard to dig. By the end of that fortnight, our lumps and blisters were callused over, and we smelt of nothing remotely human, so our cover was complete. Maybe that's why they always left us for an extra two weeks. They couldn't have us going soft again.'

Laura held us spellbound at this stage.

'It was in the fourth week that it happened. I was focused on my planting as usual. The itching had eased and so there was nothing to distract me. I felt like I was the only person on the planet. I had just finished planting a whole box of spruce trees. I straightened up, feeling quite delighted with myself, when I heard a rustling of leaves on my right. I turned to see how Tom, my planting buddy, was doing but there was no sign of him. What I did see, only yards from me, at this side of a fallen rotting tree, was a tiny brown bear nosing around in the leaves. The only time I had ever seen anything so adorable was when I visited toyshops at Christmas. You know that huge, soft, cuddly teddy you have just got to hug. Well, there he was, tossing leaves in the air with his nose. However, the urge to hug this one disappeared just as soon as I felt it. Where there's Baby Bear, you can bet your grandmother, Mammy Bear and Daddy Bear are close behind. In slow motion, I began to back away. He looked up and, without hesitation, he came bounding over to me. He looked playful enough, but with every bound, he emitted a loud bawling sound. I waved my arms at him, taking a few dummy runs in his direction, hoping to scare him without making any noise. It didn't work. He continued clambering over the branches in my direction, all the while wailing his head off. I grabbed my backpack and turned around to get out of there as fast as I could. Then, from out of nowhere, a ten-foot-tall fur coat was pawing the air, two yards in front of me. I was looking straight into these huge jaws and teeth. The roar she gave nearly blew my head off. I thought of nothing but getting to hell out of there. Can you imagine, standing there, all five feet of me, threatening a ten-foot bear? Try fooling her that you're bigger than her. What a joke! I didn't scream with the intention of scaring her. I tried to scream to get help, but not a squeak came out of my mouth. Stretching up on my tippy toes wasn't an option. I was not going to be the jelly in a Mammy and Baby Bear sandwich, and so I took off. Uphill, downhill? Upwind, downwind? I didn't have a clue. I just ran. I got my voice back because I was screaming nearly as loud as the bear was roaring behind me. I clambered over tree trunks, slid down ditches, tearing every shred of clothing. The roaring was in my ears the whole way back to camp. When I got there, I was still screeching. It was only then that I looked behind me. There was no sign of the bear.

'Tom and two others came stumbling into the camp to see if anyone was hurt. The foreman was sitting against a tree reading. I couldn't speak at first, then I went for him, bald-headed. "Why didn't you come out to help me?"

'"I heard no distress whistle. Did any of you?" He didn't even look up.

'"Didn't you hear me roaring and shouting for Christ's sake?"

'"You never blew your whistle, now did you, honey? You know the procedure. Lost or attacked, blow your whistle. They're the rules. I work by the rules. If I was to follow every roar of you city folk in the forest, I would never sit down."

'It seemed to have been a common occurrence for planters to crack up after a few weeks in the forest. Those who cracked up often screamed, except for Steve that is; he was the one who just stopped speaking.

'After that, I was the noisiest planter in the group. Any bear within a roar of me was forewarned. I sang aloud to every one of the trees that I planted. As I walked from place to place, I sang and my pots and pans jangled noisily from my backpack.

'One day each month, we got a $200 advance and the chopper suddenly appeared from over the mountains and we were lifted into the nearest hillbilly town. We never knew in advance, so it was a total shock to the system. A long hot shower, clean clothes, a pizza, a few beers and off again.

'In the long run, the hillbillies proved to be more dangerous than the bears. These outback towns are inhabited by loggers and oil pipeline men. They're macho, drunken and sex-starved, I tell you. Most bars have signs that read "No tree planters."

'Inside, usually beside the dartboard, they have another scoreboard, for the number of tree-planters who have been beaten up. The irony of it! I survived a month in the wilderness with bears and bugs, and then returned to so-called civilisation, only to be beaten up by a logger.

'My mom said, "Tell them you're doing a good thing, dear." I hadn't the heart to tell her it was *they* who thought they were doing the good thing.'

By the time Laura had finished her story, Peig's fire had burned down and only one candle flickered. The girls went to bed while they still had some light. I pulled on my boots and rainjacket and headed back out into the storm. The rain had stopped momentarily, but a clouded black sky still hid the moonlight. Thunder rolled in the northern sky. Then there was silence as I counted the seconds before the sky suddenly crackled and flashed. The whole sky to the north lit up. For a few moments, the ruins of the crumbling Blasket village below me flashed a steel grey. The thunder and lightning continued. Fascinated, I set off up the north path behind Peig's house towards the cliffs for a better look. The torch was weak and, between lightning flashes, I just managed to make out my footsteps. At the brow of the hill, the thunder rolled again. I counted, waiting in the darkness. Suddenly, with a jagged burning tear, the heavens shattered. A ripple of angry fire split the clouds, piercing the belly of the Sleeping Giant. The shock electrified the whole island, bathing the dead man in an eerie blue light before the sky was plunged into darkness once more. I shut my eyes tight, yet I could see him. The man of death was back, hauling his great bulk from the water to tower above the sky. Panic-stricken, I cowered on my hands and knees. In the storm, my terrors returned. A madwoman severing the limbs off her husband. The dead man, rising for revenge. A giant bear pawing the sky. Claws ripping my belly open as a wolf howls in my throat. The stench of blood and death on my skin. I retched helplessly as I clung to the wet grass.

While the storm raged, terror and shock jolted through my body. Gradually, I became aware of myself, lying soaking wet on the ground. I had let fear win once more. I had made it through the sea arch that morning, yet already I had lost myself to fear again. Anger suddenly overwhelmed me. For too long, my days and nights had been spent living the night-mares of a dead man. At last I understood that the horror was not mine and I wanted it no longer. I cursed the bastard in the blackness and hurled every rock I could find over the cliffs towards the Sleeping Giant. I battled against the darkness until I had no energy left to move.

Eventually the storm burned out and the eastern sky began to dilute the darkness to a powdery opaqueness. Exhausted, I stumbled back down from the cliffs into the silent obscurity of an old charcoal drawing of the village. The hostel was closed and sleeping. The silhouettes of two donkeys sheltered, motionless, against the gable wall. I slipped silently inside the hut before the island awoke.

Moontime

For the next three nights, electrical storms danced over the Blasket Islands. Seemingly oblivious to them, the Sleeping Giant rested peacefully once more. The ferries disappeared over to shelter in Dingle and so the Great Blasket Island was left in peace too. Each night, despite the thunder and lightning, I slept deeply. Each day, I avoided company and remained close to the hut, still feeling drained and shaken. On the fourth night the skies cleared and a huge full moon sailed above the last few fleeting clouds.

During that night, groaning and wailing awoke me. I had never heard anything like it before. The strangest chorus filled the air. I followed the sound in the direction of the beach, climbed down and watched, unseen, from the moon shadows of the rocks. The full moon had drawn over fifty seals from the sea. Each wave offered another glistening body to the milky light until they became one live, shimmering mass on the White Strand. Their yelps and barks carried on the night air. I saw the huge bulk of a bull seal patrolling offshore, while three seal cows surfed on the silver breakers. The bull watched until a younger female emerged from around the rocky headland. She hesitated, sensing the attention of the male, who was stretching his snout into the night sky. She responded by throwing back her head, showering sparkling droplets of water into the air.

Simultaneously they dived, arching black backs into the moonlight as they slid underwater. They re-emerged just a few yards apart. Then the female approached, trailing in her wake a shimmering veil of phosphorescence. In a sudden burst of spray, the male was beside her, sinking his muzzle into her neck as they merged into the darkness of the sea. Spiralling back through the surface, their necks were locked together while their tails interlaced, thrashing the water in a rhythmic frenzy. Suspended in streams of moonlight, they mated, their duet reverberating on the rocks and echoing through the ruins.

When they drifted apart, the female hauled herself out of the waves, rolling onto the sand, full and sated. She folded into the moon chorus that continued on the beach, and was gone. Exhilarated, I climbed quietly back through the shadows to the clifftop and returned to bed.

Next morning the presence of the seals charmed the island. They lay on the far end of the White Strand, bathing their dappled-marble and oil-black bodies in the sunshine. Laura and Sigrid watched from inside the half-door. The three visitors staying in the hostel moved around quietly, speaking in hushed tones, as they established distant vantage points.

The Harvard student set up her tripod amongst the ruins, watching patiently for a stretch, a gaping yawn or a flick of flippers.

A young Tipperary couple went to the far cliff. The girl sat fascinated, sketching the basking colony. The boy lay on his front, watching her with an equal degree of wonder.

In my sheltered cove at the village end of the beach, I waded gently into the water. I cupped my hands and poured the water over my upturned face. It streamed cold and glistening down my hair and body. I traced the undulating surface of the water back and forth with my palms as I gazed at the seals in the distance. The memory of the moonlight dance was palpable in the water as I slid silently beneath.

From the water, I could see Sue, back up on the island, standing motionless outside her yellow door. She looked in the direction of the seals. The only movement was the dance of the red wool scarf in her busy hands.

The whole island focused on the beach, mesmerised by the majesty of the sea creatures.

Suddenly, three male figures hurled themselves into the picture, flinging their backpacks onto the sand as they jostled and shouted. Then a squat, bald man amongst them swaggered down the beach towards the colony. He didn't stop, he didn't pause. He advanced towards the seals. Shocked, the whole island held its breath. We could not call out. We could not warn them. The man was yards away. Still the seals did not move. Suddenly, the spell was broken. A violent shudder electrified the body of seals until they became a pulsating mass.

Three seals broke loose and rippled into the surf. A surge of dark bodies spilled after them. The water seethed with life, then, just as quickly, melted the sleek creatures to nothing. The sea glimmered, quiet and empty. We watched in stunned silence.

The bald man stood at the water's edge, legs apart and hands on his hips. Suddenly, he roared at the top of his voice, beating his breast, then turned, flexing his muscles for a friend's camera. The harsh shouts and laughter of the men rasped on the morning air. As the sunshine and ferries returned, the island had lost its peace once more.

The Blasket village on the east side of the island, with the White Strand below.

The Seal People

I fled like the seals as, yet again, the ferries ploughed incessantly through the Blasket Sound. Each morning, I escaped to the solitude at the end of the island. There I bird-watched, sketched and daydreamed. I ambled back as evening approached, and watched the changing shadows as the pink light seeped through the clouds, staining the sea to the west of the Great Blasket.

A few evenings after the night of the seals, I met Laura coming around the northern headland. 'Was my curry that bad? We haven't seen you for days,' she called.

'No, it was delicious. I stupidly went for a walk in the storm afterwards, and got soaked. Even lost my torch. Ended up with a right chill.' She looked at me dubiously. 'Honestly, I stayed in the bunk for three days.'

'Gee, you do some crazy things.' She was gathering bunches of dry heather, from which she said that she intended to make a sweeping brush for the cafe. 'Only thing, I can't find is a branch as a broom handle,' she sighed.

'You won't find one either. There's not a tree on the island.'

'I know, and we've burned every piece of driftwood.'

We strolled to the Seal Cove, racking our brains for a solution to the broom handle. That was soon forgotten about as we lay on the clifftop watching the seal pup suckling the huge, dappled cow. The contented rhythmic flapping of his flippers was the same, but Junior was barely recognisable: he was easily three times his original size.

'He'll soon be swimming off,' Laura said. 'Seán thinks that it could be in the next day or two.'

'Well, I hope to God he doesn't end up scampering up onto the White Strand, at the mercy of the hordes of tourists and dogs on it lately.' I was still upset, thinking of the bald man scaring away the seals.

'I don't think you need worry about that. The seals won't come within an ass's roar of the beach from now on until the boats stop running, in the fall.'

'Did you see that fool driving the seals off the beach the other morning?'

'Yeah. Complete barbarian, wasn't he? Seán tackled the three of them when they came up looking for beers. All they did was laugh in his face. I had to go outside, I was that mad. Still, if I had been the one to serve them, they would never forget it: they would have gotten one gut-twisting sandwich.'

'Pity you didn't serve them.'

'Seals are so harmless; it's hard to understand anyone wanting to harm them.'

'Well, if your livelihood is at stake, you try and find something to blame. Drift-netting, over-fishing and corruption appear to be out of the small fisherman's control, so he vents his frustration on something tangible, like the seal. A fisherman told me that they used to poison them with strychnine, but after that was banned, brake fluid and home-made bombs were used. Up until the seventies, there was a bounty of three pounds per snout paid. Often you'll come across one with a bullet hole in it.'

Laura looked at me aghast. 'God, that's totally gross. How can you hurt something that looks so human? Gee, at times, I think the Beverley Sisters look more human than seal.'

'Well, it's said they were human once. Have you ever heard of the seal people?'

'You mean people who were suckled by seals as babies?' Without waiting for an answer, she continued. 'I heard a cool story about a baby left in a cave for safety while its mother was gathering seaweed on the Gravel Strand. When she came back to collect the infant, the tide had come in and covered the mouth of the cave. She was reassured that the baby would be fine, up on the high rock for the next six hours. It would just be hungry. Anyway, according to the story, the weather turned stormy. The seas were huge for the next four days, leaving the cove inaccessible. On the fifth day, the men went down to retrieve the body of the dead baby, if it hadn't already been swept out by the tide. When the water was low enough, the father waded into the cave first, followed by the others. The rock where the infant had been stowed was drenched with pools of seawater and seaweed; it had obviously been submerged during the storm and there was no trace of the baby. Then a movement caught the man's attention in the depths of the cave, where a seal was hauled out, high on the gravel above the tide, suckling her young. As the men startled her, she escaped into the water, leaving her young behind. When the man waded over, he found not a seal pup, but his own baby daughter, alive and well. She was warm and full of milk. The seal had pushed the helpless child up above the tide line, nursing it through the storm. Imagine that.'

'I heard of something like that happening on the Hebrides too.'

'There, it's gotta be true,' Laura said. 'Why, in the name of heaven, would any mother make up a story like that about her own baby? One sure way to get the kid bullied at school. We've got similar stories of babies suckled by wolves in Canada, like in *The Jungle Book*. It's a maternal instinct, I reckon.'

We watched the seal suckling her pup far below. Neither of us spoke for a while, then Laura rolled over onto her back in the sunshine and asked, 'So what are seal people supposed to be?'

'Apparently they could take seal or human shape. According to legend, when Noah's Ark was full, the people who were left behind turned into seals. One of the fishermen told me a story about seal people on the Great Blasket.'

'If it's good, you're invited to dinner. Well, on condition that you don't go to ground again for a whole week.'

I promised her that I wouldn't. She cradled her head in her lower arm and adjusted her baseball cap, in order to see me, and at the same time shield her eyes from the sun. I sat, keeping the seal in view and began a story for my supper.

'Peadar was an islander in his late forties. He had no wife. He had lost his eye as a child and with it his appeal to girls. The Blasket people thought that he was a lost cause, so it was a great surprise when he arrived back into the island one night with a wife.

'From the very start the islanders thought that Niamh was strange. She looked foreign, with a dusky complexion, huge dark eyes and sleek, shiny, black hair. She kept to herself and Peadar was tight-lipped when any question was put to him about the origins of his bride. Still, whatever people thought, everyone agreed that Peadar and Niamh made a most contented couple.

'They said that she had strange ways about her. She wore

layers of long, shapeless skirts and shawls, always covering her arms and hands. The children used to say that she had no hands. She rarely went walking since it seemed to be difficult for her. She took small, shuffling steps and when she did go out, it was at night. Some talked cruelly behind her back about her looks and her strange habits. Kinder people suggested that it was such talk that forced the poor woman to venture forth alone and at night.

'When darkness fell, and the sound of seals wailing and surf breaking filled the island, she went walking. She would walk the paths and watch the sea, but never went to the beach. In eight years, nobody ever saw her on the beach.

'A few months after her arrival, Nan Cleary told the women to stop their gossiping and to be civil to the dark woman. Then, one Sunday, Nan invited her to come and pray the Rosary with the women in the National School. That was the custom while the menfolk were across on the mainland at mass. Peadar said that his wife would go and so she did. It was Niamh's sweet singing that held the women spellbound and won them over. The thrill of her voice struck every listener to the depths of their soul. Once the women of the island had accepted her, it would be a brave man who would utter a word against her.

'A year later, Peadar was the happiest man alive when she gave birth to their healthy baby boy. Peadar gave Niamh the gift of a beautiful soft wool shawl. It was woven with jade, green and turquoise wool and shimmered like the sea. From that day she was never seen without it.

'Like his mother, Éanna had dark skin and deep, inkwell eyes. Like his father, he was strong and tall. The young boy grew like any island boy, except for one affliction. He was afraid of the water. He never went to the beach to run on the sand or to play hurling like the others. Of all the young boys of his age, he was the strongest at hauling turf and stones. He was the fastest, climbing steep slopes with heavy loads of seaweed to fertilise the potatoes. He was the fittest boy, rounding up sheep on the hills. When other boys were puffing and blowing, there wasn't one quick breath from Éanna. All this was well and good, but not enough for a man making his future on the Great Blasket Island. He had to be able to fish and to man a *naomhóg*. Peadar understood the boy's limitations and so he encouraged Éanna to succeed with his schooling. Perhaps with the boy's kindness and angelic voice, he would be destined for the priesthood. Then the sea would no longer be a worry for his mother. So by the time that the boy was seven years old, he outshone every thirteen-year-old scholar in the schoolroom. Éanna, like his mother, had a most beautiful and haunting voice. When they sang together, it was said that the seals and birds came in to shore to listen.

'During that year, Éanna and four other young boys were being groomed for their First Holy Communion. The whole island seemed to be preparing with them. You would have thought that the mothers themselves were making the Holy Communion with all the fuss that was going on. They were so involved because when the actual day would come, only the men would cross to Dún Chaoin with the boys for the mass.

'Éanna was as excited as any of the children. Niamh, however, was anxious and distracted for weeks. Peadar was distressed, seeing her like this, and he reassured her every day. She would not be consoled until the event was over and their son had returned safely into the island. On the First Holy Communion Sunday, the men set off early in the boats. Niamh stood on the clifftop that May morning, her sea-green shawl wrapped tightly around her. She watched the boats until they became tiny black dots, swallowed by the shadows of the mainland cliffs. She remained there while the women went to and from the National School for the Rosary and while they returned to their houses and cooked the Sunday meal. She kept to herself all day.

'Over on the mainland, the First Holy Communion had gone off famously. The five island children received the sacrament with the children of Dún Chaoin and Ballyferriter. After the mass, the priest spoke to all the island boys outside the church. Once each had received the priest's blessing, the men made haste back to the slipway.

'Peadar and three other men took to the oars in one boat. Éanna and his two young friends sat up in the bow. They were full of high spirits. When they were a good mile out to sea, they were suddenly surrounded by seals. The three men swore that in all their days fishing, they had never seen so many seals. The boys squealed with delight, barking and yelping at the shiny bald heads. Éanna lost his fear of the water, leaning over to touch the seals with the others. The seals were fearless and nuzzled the hands of the boys. Peadar became mad with fright, roaring at the seals and lashing out with the oar at them. He screamed at Éanna to sit down. The other men were as captivated as the boys were, and with all the excitement and commotion, Peadar's appeals were ignored. The boys whooped with joy. It was during all this confusion that Éanna leaned too far overboard, stroking two sleek seals. After each contact they drifted farther out of the boy's reach. Nobody could explain how it happened that Éanna slid into the water so easily after the two seals. Without the slightest splash, the lips of the water closed over the young boy and the seals. It all seemed to have happened before anyone could react.

'Peadar screamed for the boy, making the boat rock dangerously as he stumbled from side to side, searching desperately. The men scanned the waters, but Éanna never resurfaced. As quickly as the seals had appeared, they disappeared into the green waters. For hours the men searched the area but found no trace of Éanna.

'Before the boats had come close to the island, the women knew that something terrible had happened. The crying of the boys and the frantic wailing of Peadar filled the Blasket Sound. It was a hard job the men had to do to prevent Peadar from jumping in after his son, on the journey back to the Blasket. When the boats landed, the awful truth was broken to the women. The neighbours ran ahead to be with Niamh; her heart would wrench in two with the news. The door was wide open but the cottage was empty. The islanders searched her usual haunts but there was no sign of her. Once Peadar realised that his wife was missing, he raced as fast as the wind straight down onto the White Strand. Nobody could keep up with him. When the people reached the cliff overlooking the strand, they saw Peadar crumpled to his knees in the shallow ripples. He clutched the jade and turquoise shawl to his chest. No one would ever forget the heartbreaking wailing of the man screaming to the waves.'

Laura said nothing for a while when I had finished. Then she sighed and said, 'What happened to Peadar?'

'Well, he never spoke about the loss of his wife and child. In the months that followed, he kept to himself, taking on the strange habits of his wife. He walked the cliffs here by the Seal Cove at night, listening to the singing of the seals. He lived like that for three years and then he died one winter's night, out on the cliffs alone.'

We sat on the grass, watching a brilliant orange orb sink into the horizon beyond An Téaracht. Seventy or eighty metres below us, the full tide surged onto the gravel. The scalloped lace ripples glowed with orange light. Slowly the seal cow began to nudge the pup towards the frothy bubbles.

He seemed reluctant at first. He stopped as the first wave flooded around him and drained back through the gravel. The next wave came quickly, floating him for an instant. He looked to his mother for reassurance. She was by his side, urging him along with her. As the third wave broke, she dipped her head and slid beneath it. The pup hesitated, was upended and then dived after his mother. The sleek heads of mother and son reappeared beyond the breakers.

'Good luck, you guys!' Laura called after them. I could say nothing, fearing that my voice would fail me. We watched until the seals had disappeared and the last droplet of molten sun had dissolved into the sea. In the dusk, my tears fell silently. Laura was on her feet already. 'You're not supposed to cry at your own story, you big softie. Come on. Éanna has just earned you dinner.'

A Day in the Weaver's

Friday was the quietest day on the Great Blasket Island during the summertime. Out on the mainland, it was changeover day. Tourists were busy loading cars and setting off on long journeys home while others were excitedly heading to the Dingle Peninsula to take their places. The beaches were quieter while the roads were busier. From the sanctuary of the sea, the Great Blasket Island gave a shrug of relief, watching the chain of colourful matchbox cars glint in the sunshine as it snaked around Slea Head. During the Friday swop-over, only one ferry operated between Dún Chaoin and the Great Blasket Island.

'How would you like a day minding the shop?' Sue asked as she popped her head through my door one Thursday evening. 'It should be quiet tomorrow, so I'm going out to the mainland for next month's supplies. I'll show you where I leave the key and you can help yourself to tea, scones and whatever you like.'

Without waiting for a response, she continued with the arrangements and explained the schedule for the following day. I did not know how to say no. That had always been a problem for me. It was different, however, with Sue's request; she was asking something perfectly reasonable of me, something any normal person could do and something she was entitled to ask. After all, she had given me huge support since my arrival on the island whether she was aware of it or not.

Three things terrified me. Firstly, the prospect of meeting so many people. The familiar company of Laura and Sigrid was one thing, but a shop full of strangers was another matter entirely. Secondly, the thought that I would be in a situation that I could not get away from. What if I panicked? Thirdly, there was my lack of any mathematical sense.

I knew that it was time to move out into the world again. Here was a challenge I would have to meet. 'I'm afraid I'm not a great accountant, Sue,' I answered smiling, although my stomach was churning with anxiety.

'Don't worry, everything is priced clearly. I'll show you. Before I realised it, we were walking down the path to her yellow door. 'If anyone wants tea and a scone, charge one-twenty. There's change in the box.'

A shaft of evening sunlight filtered dancing dust particles inside her door. My friendly robin pecked at the floor within the beam of light. As we stepped inside, he hopped indifferently past my foot, foraging for abandoned crumbs. The room was filled with the golden warmth of baking scones.

I knelt and nudged a currant towards him.

'You've met then!' Sue smiled.

'Yes, every dawn. I think I must be first on his rounds.'

'Is he still at that? He used to waken Ray Stagles every morning too.'

'He's fairly bedraggled-looking today, isn't he?'

'Looks like you've been in the wars, my friend. What have you been fighting about?'

The robin cocked his head as if considering his answer, then hopped out of the spotlight in under a wooden chair, which was laden with woollen shawls, to continue his quest for food.

'Now, the price is on everything: shawls, scarves, hats, tablemats, rugs, everything.' As I looked around, I could not see a free inch of wall space. Rugs, woven wall hangings and scarves hung all over. Chairs, countertop, windowsills, even the leaking gas fridge was piled high with garments. The kitchen table was lost under Páid's woodcraft. Maps of the island and postcards covered the tiny table inside the door and every shape and style of woollen hat hung from shelves, nails and cupboard knobs. A narrow path wove its way through the mountains of wool to the back wall, where Sue had just enough room to stand in front of the old gas cooker. 'Tea and coffee are here, over the cooker. I keep two kettles on the go. Sugar and jam in here,' she said, indicating shelves hidden behind a red velvet curtain. Everything that could be was secured in jars, while other items hung from the ceiling, out of the reach of greedy mice. 'Milk and butter are in the fridge.' I wondered at the best line of approach to the fridge door, which was concealed by the loom and three giant towers of wool.

'There's a notebook here where I record each item I sell. Don't worry if you don't sell anything. Most people just come in for a rest, a good look around and a chat.'

'Well, I certainly hope I manage to sell something for you. Remind me about the dyes again. I'll have to be able to tell people where the natural colours come from.'

'Right but, again, don't *worry* if you can't remember them. The wall hanging nailed to the timber over there has most of the dyes in it. This rich tan is from onion skins. The green below it is from nettles. The gold colour comes from grey lichen – you know the one I was collecting off the rocks the other day?'

'Yes. So that means the gold in this hat comes from lichen.' I thought I was getting the hang of it.

'No, that actually came from another onion dye. These rusts and reddish colours come from heather, and these blends of greens are from mosses.'

I was lost. Each colour seemed to have an endless number of shades. 'But how can the rock lichen give so many different colours? That one is gold and this one is almost red.'

'Depending on the season, iodine and algae occur in varying amounts in the sea. Lichens are filter feeders, so, as the composition of the water changes, the lichen changes. The different phases of the moon and the tides will affect it too. That means that, with home dyes, it's impossible to match colours exactly. If I have weed or lichen left over and I boil it a few days later, the colour can be different from the first batch. It can have dried out and lost its potency or I might have boiled it for a longer or shorter time, changing the colour that way.'

I had visions of a four-seasons' jumper: four batches of island wool, each dyed from rock lichen picked during each of the different seasons. Then I saw the colour that I wanted as winter. 'How do you get this deep purple?' I asked.

'Commercial dye, I'm afraid. It's nearly impossible to get purple naturally. That's why purple was the colour of kings in the past, the most elusive and, therefore, the most expensive colour.'

I put back the purple shawl, feeling disappointed.

'If you saw this red colour being made on the island in the past, you knew that a young woman was emigrating. Your red petticoat was like your rite of passage, I suppose.'

I had one last look around before the evening light

disappeared. Sue started the fire with an empty milk carton and flour bag. 'Don't forget to remind people to take their litter back home to the mainland. The island is a plastic-free zone, so don't take any.'

'Right, now you'd better get your red petticoat ready for the morning.' I gave her my shopping list: matches, candles, bananas, apples, brown rice, vegetables, beans and batteries.

'I'll knock on your door before I leave and thanks very much; I couldn't go unless I had someone to look after the shop.'

'Thank me when I've sold something. Goodnight.'

The next morning, things happened so fast: as soon as I waved Sue off on the ferry, I lit the gas under two kettles, put the spinning wheel out on the wall and attempted to hang the weathered, wooden signs for the weaver's shop outside on the gable. The few rusty nails, jutting from the wall at odd angles, failed to hold the heavy battered boards, which read '*Fáilte Isteach*', 'Craft Shop' and 'Visitors Welcome'. In the hands of any geometrically minded person, the rusty chains dangling from each sign would have matched the rusty nails on the wall. I was not that person. As soon as I had one side up, the other would fall down. As the kettle screeched, I dashed inside, momentarily abandoning the task. The scones looked delicious, so I decided that it would be time for breakfast, once the sign was up. I lit a nightlight under some lavender oil, then re-emerged into the glare of the sunshine.

The spinning wheel looked spectacular, standing high on the stone wall, cutting brilliant blue slices of sky. I turned back to my battered sign, reaching up on my tiptoes, when a man's voice startled me. 'Let me help you with that.' A tall figure stretched above me, hooking the two chains easily into place. 'Which one is next?' he asked in a strong Scottish accent. Awkwardly I handed him '*Fáilte Isteach*' just as two great, sweating American women collapsed in a heap onto one of the benches. Behind them, a steady procession was making slow progress up from the landing slip. I had not noticed the ferry's arrival. My heart started racing. A wave of nausea surged through me. I didn't think I could do it.

'Can we have two Cokes with ice, dear?' one of the large ladies asked, before I had even thanked the man who had hung the signs.

'I have only tea and coffee. For Coke, you'll have to go up to the cafe. This is the weaver's shop.' I pointed in the direction of the cafe; up the hill towards the *Dáil* and across the rabbit path. They looked at me in horror.

'I think we have walked quite enough, Dorothy, don't you? We'll take two coffees,' she panted.

At this stage, there were three French girls inside, trying on hats. A young boy emerged with a map and handed me a fiver. As I made to go inside to get his change, a man shouted over the wall, 'Can you tell me which house is Tomás Ó Croimhthain's please?'

I indicated the ruin, set back to the left of Páidí Dunleavy's cottage, smiled and headed for the door once more.

'So where did Muiris Ó Súilleabháin live?' he asked. I went out through the gap in the wall, pointing out the ruin at the back of Sue's, still holding the fiver. I had no sooner shown him that house than he asked for the King's house.

'We sell a very good map and guide, if you'd like it.'

'No, thank you,' his wife interrupted. 'We've wasted enough money this holiday. We'll wait till you're ready.'

The tall Scottish man was still there, gazing over the island.

'We'll have cake with the coffees,' the larger of the American ladies added as I walked past.

'How much for this, please?' The three French girls held out one postcard to me. I took the card, escaping inside to find the price, get the boy change and make the coffees. I stopped in panic. Differently priced baskets of hats were emptied and strewn everywhere. I had no idea which hat belonged to which basket. I attempted to put order on it and make coffees as two Cork ladies came in. They were fascinated with the natural dyes. I explained as much as I had gleaned from Sue. Before re-emerging with the coffees, I had sold two scarves, two maps and a postcard each to five children. I came into the sunshine, relieved; I had sold something! As I set the milk and sugar on the upended box and presented two steaming mugs of coffee and a plate of scones to my customers, I felt quite proud of myself. I offered the tall man a cup of tea and thanked him for his help. Just then, I overheard one of the Americans commenting on my bare feet. I paused as she continued.

'It couldn't be hygienic, making food like that.'

'The whole place is primitive. I don't understand how the receptionist would be allowed recommend *this* as a trip.'

The Scottish man smiled reassuringly at me. 'I'd love a cup of tea, thank you, and those scones look great. Sarah, come over for some tea!' A young girl, who was kneeling patiently outside a rabbit hole, looked up.

'I think he's gone out the back door, Dad.' She looked about twelve, fair-skinned and fair-haired. Her shoulders and nose were going pink already. As I made a pot of tea, I could hear her chattering. 'I've counted eleven rabbits already, Dad. There are holes everywhere. Look at the two donkeys over there, at that funny house with the round top. Can I feed them?' The doorway darkened as more visitors came in. They stopped immediately, allowing their eyes to adjust. A man in an Australian hat – the kind with corks on strings – stood in the doorway with a woman and children.

'*Dia dhuit*,' was all I could understand as he spoke to me at full speed. I apologised once more for my lack of Irish. 'No need to apologise, I didn't let you get a word in.' Liam introduced himself and his family. He was a lecturer in University College Cork and was a frequent visitor to the island.

Another older couple came in, speaking Irish too. I could just pick up that they were from Cashel, County Tipperary, as I hurried in and out with teapots and mugs. They held Joan and Ray Stagles's book open and were trying to find Tomás Ó Croimhthain's house on the map. Taking care not to drop jam on the page, I pointed it out.

Outside, while I poured the tea, introductions were made. The lady from Cashel was fascinated with Tomás Ó Croimhthain, recalling how he never married the girl that he truly loved, because his sister did not think it was a suitable match. Liam suggested that it was Tomás Ó Criomhthain who had given us the truest account of island life because he had spent all seventy-one years of his life on the island. Peig, on the other hand, was by birth a mainlander, only coming to the island after her wedding. Muiris Ó Súilleabháin had left the island and spent most of his life in the city. As I went in and out serving, clearing and selling, I picked up snatches of the conversation, which switched between Irish and English.

When the next ferry came into sight, the American women who had been watching for it through my binoculars stood up to leave. 'Well, this was a waste of a morning. There's nothing to see out here.'

'Bunratty Castle was much better. Where is the restroom, dear?'

'Sorry there's none here. You'll have to go up to the cafe.' They looked at me in disdain. Once again, my bare feet seemed to be the focus of attention.

'I think we might just wait till we get back to the hotel, Dorothy.' Without another word, they brushed past me and began stepping sideways heavily down the hill. I was still smarting from their dismissal as Sarah's father strode down the hill past them, retrieving two backpacks that were lying abandoned at the clifftop.

'Goodbye, ladies,' he called. 'What a pity you can't stay over. Maybe next year!'

Meanwhile, Sarah was delighted to carry mugs and plates in and out for me. Washing up in a basin, out on the grass, was her idea of 'heaven'. She told me that she and Michael, her father, had been on the island before when she was very small, but she did not remember. Her mother had been with them then. She asked me if she could help for a while. I told her I would be delighted, if her father did not mind, but it would be a shame to lose out on seeing the island too.

'We're staying for a few days, so I've got lots of time.'

After three pots of tea and much chat, the Cashel couple decided to leave. 'Can you suggest a walk for us? We need to be back for the four o'clock ferry.' I did not realise it at the time, but it was to be the first of countless walks that I would tailor to suit visitors during my stay on the island.

Liam and his family left to explore the village, while Sarah and her father went up the hill to drop their bags in Peig's hostel. Dozens of groups and couples filed in and out during the morning. By one o'clock, I was exhausted and there was no respite. I had become historian, tour guide, walk planner, tea-maker, first aider and listener to family trees. I wondered at Sue's stamina.

'Where's Peig's house?'

'Do you have a book of wild flowers of the island?'

'Can you show me where Tomas Crow Hane lives? He's dead? No!'

'Do you take Visa?'

'Where do you live? How long do you stay out here?'

'How long will it take me to walk around the island?'

'Do you know which cottage Charlie Haughey lives in?'

'Can you show me where Peig's son fell off the cliff?'

'Can I buy a holiday house out here?'

'Who owns the island?'

'Do you pray a lot out here?'

'Can you show me how the spinning wheel works?'

'Gee, it's dark in here. Can you turn on the light, ma'am? You gotta be kiddin'! Marcia, this lady's got no electricity. Can you believe that?'

'You mean you've gotten no television, period? How can you live?'

I escaped into the blazing sunshine with yet another tray of teas, leaving Al and Marcia hunting for light switches.

'You're keeping busy?' Páidí smiled at me from outside the wall. Páid, with the smiling blue eyes, was beside him. 'We're in collecting the wool.'

'Come in and have a cup of tea.'

The two men leaned on the wall and looked out across the Blasket Sound while I returned inside.

'You're a Fennelly, aren't you?'

'I am,' I answered the silhouette by the window.

'I'm Martin O'Halloran from Callan. Whose daughter are you then?'

'Frank was my father. Did you know him?'

'Of course.' As I made the tea, we talked of my father, my brother William, the farm, and of Callan. After a few minutes, another man handed me money for some postcards and introduced himself.

'Tim O'Sullivan. I think I know one of your uncles. Nial?'

A Day in the Weaver's

When he told me that he worked with the Department of Finance, I became even more addled, calculating change. I couldn't subtract and talk at the same time. In fact, I couldn't even do the former to start with, so with the help of Tim, from the Department of Finance, change was issued to all in the shop in record time. More and more people filed in and out of the tiny room, each a fresh wave from another place.

By mid-afternoon I was punch drunk. I slumped on the edge of a bench by Páid and Páidí, watching the steady stream of visitors enter and leave the doorway. Only as one emerged, holding up an item enquiringly, did I volunteer my services.

'That's it; you have to pace yourself. It's like drinking pints,' a great stomach of a man winked at me, as he melted on the other bench in the sunshine. I smiled, flopping back down with a mug of water. 'Tell me what happened to that rusty ol' wreck that used to be on Coumenoule Beach?' he asked.

I remembered the wreck but knew nothing about it. Páidí filled in all the facts.

'They removed it for the shooting of that Tom Cruise film in 1991. It was a Spanish boat on its maiden voyage from Spain to Iceland, ran aground there, at the foot of the cliffs, in a storm in 1982.'

'Was there loss of life?' a German lady with impeccable English asked.

'No, thank God. All fifteen crew were airlifted off.'

'Are there many wrecks off the islands here?'

'There are. Not so many in recent years, but a lot in the old days.'

'On your way back, you'll cross over the wreck of one of the Spanish Armada ships.'

'There must be very little of it remaining. That was in the 1500s I believe.'

'That's right. It was November 1588,' Páidí said.

'When I came across to the island, the ferryman located the exact spot for someone, using the GPS. The ship was called the *Santa Maria Della Rosa*. It's lying in about thirty-five metres of water just southeast of what he called the Stromboli Reef.' I pointed to where I thought it was.

Páidí corrected me, indicating a point farther east and continued. 'There's not much to see now, but the odd dive boat still goes out. They say there's ballast, pewter, arquebuses and shot still lying around.'

The three German ladies looked out over the sparkling water to where Páidí had pointed.

The large, sweating man was not impressed. 'And what would you be wanting to dive into thirty-five metres of freezing cold water for, in the name o' Jaysus, with nothing to see but a lump of ol' ballast? By God, there must have been hundreds drowned.'

'There was only one survivor off the *Santa Maria*: a young boy who managed to swim to shore into the island here,' Páidí said.

'For all the good it did him. Didn't they hand him over to the authorities on the mainland, and he was hanged,' Páid added quietly, as he stared out to sea.

'It is difficult to imagine a storm, looking at the sea now.' The German lady who spoke introduced herself as Karin Urbach. Her friends were Franke and Brigitte. While I served them coffees, they continued to talk of wrecks with Páidí and Páid.

'I have read *The Islandman* by Tomás Ó Croimhthain,' she told her friends while still speaking in English, so as to include the men. 'He talks of the wrecks that the First World War brought into the shore as salvation for the islanders. Barrels of tea, flour, spices, cotton and even palm oil were washed ashore. They were able to trade with these, even if they didn't use them themselves.'

'That's right,' Páidí said. 'Some of the wreckage from the *Luisitania* herself was washed up here.'

'There was the body of an officer too, wasn't there?' I asked.

'There was, and it was Muiris Ó Súilleabháin who found it.'

'Páidí, what's the big house on the mainland there which looks like a church of some kind?' I had wondered about it for a while.

'That's the Cranberries' house in Dún Chaoin. It just sold for a million.'

'Oh, may I see?' Brigitte, who had been the quietest of the three, took the binoculars. Everyone took it in turns to have a look. An American teenager came out of the door and asked where Tom Cruise's house was. As I tried to explain that the house had been built only for the film *Far and Away* and that Tom Cruise did not actually have a house in Kerry, Páidí and Páid waved and set off down to the *clochán* to gather up the wool.

'What is that tower at the top of the hill?' asked a returning walker.

'It's a Napoleonic tower, built in the nineteenth century. It was —'

'What's that movie Robert Mitchum starred in? It was set here,' the American girl's mother interrupted.

'That was *Ryan's Daughter*', I said. For once I wished that I had a watch. Where was Sue's ferry? How could it take so long?

'That's right. He and Sarah Miles had sex in a bed of bluebells. It was awesome.'

'That wasn't Robert Mitchum,' her husband said.

'Honey, you know nothing about movies. It *was* Robert Mitchum. I saw every movie that gorgeous man ever starred in.'

'It was not Robert Mitchum,' he muttered, adjusting his baseball cap.

'It was Robert Mitchum!' Her voice was shrill.

'It was *not* Robert Mitchum.'

'No, and I suppose it was not you who drove on the wrong side of the road into that Dingle roundabout either, was it?' She was screaming with rage. 'It was Sarah Miles and Robert Mitchum making out in the bluebells.' Her voice was startling. This was followed by dead silence in the shop, for the first time that day. The three German ladies looked awkwardly into their coffees, while two walkers made an about-turn at the entrance.

I broke the silence. 'It was actually Sarah Miles and Christopher Jones making love in the bluebells. It was not Robert Mitchum,' I said as I headed in with some empty mugs. When I dared to come back out, the couple and their daughter had left, and the German ladies were packing up to leave.

'That was rather brave of you,' Karin announced laughing. 'I wouldn't like to be her husband on the way across. We might wait for the next ferry; it looks like there will be another at six.'

The American woman's angry words faded over the side of the cliff and we breathed a sigh of relief. Gradually, the visitors filtered down through the ruins to the landing slip. Their tideline was visible in the form of abandoned plastic bottles and a red chocolate wrapper, tumbling lazily along the path.

'Should we leave now? Perhaps this one is the last.' Franke asked anxiously.

'No, you're all right,' I called. 'Sue didn't come over on that one, so there's definitely another. Anyway, there's more than a ferryload on the slipway. You've got another hour.'

'That's great. I'm going to have a walk on the beach,' Karin announced, while the Franke and Brigitte decided to relax in the sunshine. I began to clear and wash up. Then I caught up on my sales entries in Sue's little notebook. The maps had sold out like the scones. I had sold quite a few wool garments and was delighted with my achievement. One or two stragglers appeared and bought postcards as they hurried down to the slipway. As the blue and white ferry *Oileán na nÓg* motored towards the island, a man strode back down the hill towards the shop.

'Mind if I take a photo of the spinning wheel?' he asked.

'Fire ahead.'

The man went into the little yard and snapped the spinning wheel from different angles. 'There's only a small fee,' I called over the wall as I chased a red chocolate wrapper along the path.

'And what might that be?' I was glad he was still laughing when I presented him with five plastic bottles and a ball of plastic cling film. The photographer from Real Ireland Calendars accepted the trade gallantly. Just then Karin came over the path carrying a bag full of plastic bottles and crisp bags.

'I got my trousers wet chasing this bag in and out of the waves.'

'Thank you,' the photographer said before I could say anything. 'We don't seem to be as environmentally aware as you are in Germany.'

'I do not mean to be insulting, but may I ask why Ireland is so dirty? When we arrived in Dublin, it was the first thing to shock us, and the whole countryside is similar.'

Brigitte and Franke joined us outside the wall, Brigitte adding, in slow, deliberate pronunciation, 'The plastic is like Christmas balls hanging on *sie* hedgerows in Ireland, and *sie* Irish people drop *sie* litter everywhere.'

The man nodded. 'I am not insulted, just embarrassed. It is something we are acutely aware of when we visit other European countries. We do have a huge waste problem, however. I think it is being dealt with now, because the government plans to build a number of incinerators.'

Karin looked at him in disbelief. 'But you have a tiny population. Why do you choose the worst option, and what is for us in Germany the most expensive polluter of all? Recycling seems to be unheard of in your country. People burn and dump under one's nose. There are no bottle refunds. Why there are no glass milk bottles? In Germany even Coca-Cola must have a glass bottle but in Ireland we only get plastic and more plastic.'

The photographer was at a loss for words.

'Perhaps in Ireland we have become a consumer throw-away society too fast. Environmental education and services haven't kept pace.'

'Near where we park our car there are many, many things on *sie* cliff falling to *sie* sea – fridge, mattress from beds, old cooker and much plastic bags.' Brigitte was getting more and more animated, reporting what she had seen. The photographer suggested that they all should head towards the ferry. Brigitte was not going to be distracted that easily. 'Is a very bad situation. Irish people will have big regret in *sie* future.'

I strolled down with them to give Sue a hand with the gas bottles and shopping bags. 'Thanks for taking the rubbish,' I said to Karin.

'Maybe we might write a letter to your national papers while we are here. The waste problem is like a bathtub overflowing. Experts will suggest expensive pumps, storage facilities, evaporators and goodness knows what, whereas all one has to do is turn off the tap.'

I waved goodbye to the three German ladies and the photographer. Donie the dolphin swam by the side of the dinghy as Karin clutched her plastic bag of litter. That image and that of Brigitte's cliff dump struck me as great material for the photographer's *Real Ireland* calendar but naturally, they would not feature.

'Well, how did you survive?' Sue had shed her shoes already and was loading boxes of vegetables and turf briquettes into a fish box. I loaded a backpack full of flour, sugar, meat and milk into another box, and set off at a snail's pace. By the time we had climbed up the rough ground of the slipway, I couldn't speak. We made several trips up and down, dragging full gas bottles and boxes of supplies.

'You've sold more than I would sell in a week.'

I was so surprised and delighted but exhausted after my first day, thrust into the world again. After a cup of tea and Sue's traffic report from Dingle, I felt sure that I had got the better deal that day.

The sun was sinking fast west of Inis Tuaisceart as I set off up the hill. I dropped my shopping in the hut, grabbed my sweater and pulled the door closed. The donkey was behind me, trying to get in once more. I was convinced that somewhere in her race memory she knew that her ancestors had been housed there. Nothing would satisfy her until she foaled on my bunk. I halved one of my new treasured apples and presented her with half. She knew I was hoarding the rest in my pocket and followed me, nudging my back until I gave in. As I patted her, I heard shouts and squeals over the roar of the surf. Down on the White Strand, Michael and Sarah were jumping and splashing in the waves. I was pleased that they were staying in on the island. I gave two fingers in the direction of the Sleeping Giant. Despite him, I was alive again. I smiled, hugged the sweater tightly around me and climbed up the northern path, to watch an orange sun sink into the sea.

The Rabbit's Foot

The transition from the warmth of my sleeping bag to the icy cold of the Atlantic Ocean never got easier. There was the battering by freezing waves, followed by the frenzy of breathless kicking, before my skin was adequately numbed. Then I could lie back, floating over the swell, looking back up the cliffs, into the island.

'Why do you always swim in the morning instead of the evening?' Sarah waded in towards me, hugging her arms, bouncing and wincing over every rising wave.

'Well, the reason is this. Long hair takes an age to dry, so if I bathe at night, it is soaking wet in bed, but if I bathe in the morning, it has a chance to dry.'

'My hair takes forever to dry after the sea. Much longer than after the shower. Why's that?' Like most twelve-year-old girls, Sarah had proved to be full of questions since her arrival three days before.

'Get down first; then I'll tell you.' After several attempts, she was still springing over every wave. 'Come on. One, two, three,' I urged. Eventually she was down, whooping and squealing. She dog-paddled over to me, her hair flattened, and gleaming wet down her face, like a baby otter.

'When you have seawater in your hair, it is harder to dry because it's full of salt. Salt wants to draw water to it, not let it go.'

Sarah listened as she pedalled furiously, trying to stay beside me. 'So that's why . . . Dad puts salt . . . on wine that spills,' she panted. Suddenly, spotting Donie the dolphin, she pointed excitedly, and promptly sank like a stone. As I hauled her back up, she continued to chatter. Later, up under the shelter of the cliffs, she followed my Tai Chi movements exactly, managing not to talk for a whole ten minutes.

As I said goodbye to her at the hostel, Michael popped his head out over the half-door. 'Fry-up is ready. Take a seat in the sunshine, ladies.' We sat at a weathered picnic table, towelling our hair, while the morning sun warmed our backs. Far below, Donie continued to play around the black barrels in the water. From the clifftop, outside Páidí Dunleavy's, the two donkeys made a beeline towards us, sensing there was food up for grabs.

'She's so fat, her stomach is nearly touching the ground. Look, Dad.'

'She's in foal,' I explained, pushing two pairs of velvety nostrils away from my pockets. 'We'll have three donkeys on the island any day now.' As I savoured my crispy bacon, runny eggs and toast, I was continually head-butted on the arm.

'I think that "Buzz off" needs a bit more conviction,' said Michael. He was right. These two recognised a pushover from a mile off. No wonder they arrived at my hut at seven o'clock every evening. It had nothing to do with their grazing plan. They simply knew that it was *my* dinnertime. For the second time in as many days, Michael came to my rescue. With a few sharp flicks of a tea towel and a couple of Scottish oaths, he sent the donkeys packing. They took off at a trot: a Zeppelin swaying over four matchsticks, followed by her commander, his long truncheon waving beneath him. In the fields to the north of the island, they began grazing amongst dozens of nibbling rabbits.

'Now, more tea?'

I accepted, wrapping my cold hands around the steaming mug. It was the best breakfast of my Blasket Island stay. We sat gazing out over the sparkling sea. After a while Michael broke the silence. 'You really leave everything behind when you come over here, don't you?'

'You do. You leave the drama script on the pier in Dún Chaoin.'

He nodded and smiled, his gaze fixed in the blueness.

'Do you come out here every summer?' Sarah wondered.

'No, this is only my fourth time here, but my first time staying over. The island made a huge impression on me when I was your age. I've thought about it so much over the years, it seemed to be a natural place to return to.'

'Who were you here with when you were my age?'

'My dad – like you – and my mum, my two sisters, my little brother and our dog. Then, my second time here was on a school trip when I was seventeen. Our school came here every year because we had to study the book *Peig* for our exams. Anyway, the trip that I was on was the last outing that the school ever took to the Great Blasket Island. It was a disaster.'

'Why? What did you do?' Sarah asked.

'What do you mean "what did I do"? I was a model student. I wouldn't have said "boo" to a goose.'

'To a donkey, you mean!' Michael muttered, through a mouthful of toast and honey.

'What happened? Dad, be quiet.'

'Well, about eighty of us, girls, were staying in holiday cottages in Dún an Óir. We were all fifth-year students from a school in Waterford called the Ursuline Convent. I can't remember anything about being on the mainland, except for a visit to Gallarus Oratory; that's an ancient, little stone church. You might visit it sometime. Anyway, the guide told us that we had to pass through the eye of the needle three times, in order to marry the man of our dreams.'

'What's the eye of the needle?' Sarah asked, chin cupped in her hands.

'It's a tiny window in the gable wall of the church. Well, it's tiny when you're wrapped up in a duffle coat.'

'What's a duffle coat?' After Michael had described the 1970s' standard attire, she continued, 'Did you climb through it?'

'Well I tried. As everyone was piling onto the bus, I decided to secure my future happiness. I got my head, shoulders and tummy through and that was it. My hips were wedged solid. My friend Aileen Murphy had to run for the bus driver to help her pull me back out.'

'So did you get through?'

'No. Alas, I never passed through the eye of the needle even once.'

'So did you never get married then?'

'Never. My lonely fate was sealed from that very day.'

'But why don't you try again? You're skinny. Just don't wear your coat this time.'

'Good idea. Next time, maybe. Anyway, I do remember us setting out to Peig's famous island. We were ferried across in dinghies, twelve of us to a boat. It was Easter time and the weather was fairly good, so it never occurred to us that we didn't even have one life jacket between us. It took hours to get eighty of us across. Those of us on the island were having a ball and were oblivious to the fact that anything was wrong.

'I remember finding an old black kettle, half-buried, in the ruins of one of the cottages. I was ecstatic, convinced it was Peig's. Unfortunately, the teacher pointed out Peig's house, the hostel here, which was a good distance from my find. I've tried to remember what house I'd found it in, but I can't. I've an idea that it could have been in Kearney's over there. That's the one directly below the schoolhouse, but I'm not sure. The teacher told me to leave it where I'd found it, but I carried it with me for the day.

'That teacher was Mr Cahillane, and he is the one I remember most on the island. Back at school he wore a black gown, and a page-boy hairstyle, and taught Commerce. My image of him is of his hair bouncing and his cloak billowing behind him as he strode through the corridors. He was like Batman.

'There were two female teachers with us too – Miss MacRoberts and Miss MacDonagh. Miss MacRoberts, like Batman, never taught me, but she struck me because she was very pretty and always immaculately dressed. She had fabulous curly auburn hair and always wore nail varnish. Miss MacDonagh taught us Biology. She was as excitable as a child before every single blob that we saw under the microscope. I adored her classes. We used to feel like we had found treasure with every weed that she gushed over on nature walks.

'Anyway, in the afternoon, we were all aware that there was a problem. By the time the last boatload had been dropped off on the island, it was late, and we should have been back on the mainland. The first return trip set off but halfway across the Blasket Sound the dinghy stopped, drifted, and shot off a distress flare. For some reason, this wasn't seen from the mainland, and nothing happened. We all gathered at the slipway, watching the boat drifting helplessly in the waves, and there wasn't a thing we could do about it.'

'Why didn't you use your mobile to get help?' Sarah wondered.

'Nobody had mobiles in those days. We heard later that the boat had run out of fuel. By the time a fisherman made his way out to them, and returned with fuel, over two hours had been lost. The wind blew up, the sea turned choppy and by late afternoon we were freezing cold on the island. Batman brought a big group of us walking over to the north of the island. I can still picture him tumbling head over heels down the slope in that field where the donkeys are now. I was no good at gym and painfully shy, so the sight of Mr Cahillane turning somersaults down the field with his hair flying is etched on my memory. He succeeded in distracting most of us, but there were a few girls weeping by then. I found a brilliant rabbit's foot, which upset a few more girls, but like the kettle, I was not going to part with such an amazing find.

'While all the girls were Bay City Roller fans and listened to Radio Luxembourg, under the bedcovers, I used to read James Herriot by torchlight. During holidays, I used to play my Grandad Reynolds' old seventy-eight records in the dining room, over his butcher's shop. Glenn Miller, Benny Goodman, Nelson Eddie, Mario Lanza and Doris Day were my favourites.' Sarah had heard of none of them. 'Nor had my classmates. I remember being jeered at for asking who David Essex was when I saw his poster over another girl's bed. After hearing that, my grandad tried to update me a bit, by buying me my first record, *Elvis Presley's Greatest Hits*. In one of the songs, Elvis mentions a rabbit's paw for luck. That's why I was so excited with my discovery.

'I set off to show it to Miss MacDonagh, who was back on the slipway, keeping the girls in orderly groups. She investigated the paw from every angle, concluding that the rabbit had probably died of myxomatosis. Miss MacRoberts started squealing, and told me throw the filthy thing away.'

'Did you?' Sarah asked.

'No, but my mother threw it out of my bedroom window, about three years later, when she found it.

'It began to take longer and longer between boat trips. The sea got much rougher. Then it got dark. We had to wait, huddled, in the turn of the path, halfway up from the slipway, with the teachers and the fisherman. He roared at us if we moved. It was too dark, windy and wet to go back up onto the cliffs. They were full of holes and we could be killed. Each time the dinghy returned, the night was blacker and wilder and, instead of twelve girls, eight was the most they could take. It took their best efforts to prevent the rubber dinghy from being ripped on the rocks, as they approached the slipway. Then it became too dangerous for the dinghy to even attempt to come into the landing cove, so each girl was led out over the rocks. As the wave surged in against the blackness, the ferryman struggled to manoeuvre the boat before roaring "Jump!" On the command, the fisherman literally threw the next girl into the darkness and the spray.

'After some hours, there were ten of us students, three teachers and the fisherman remaining. He roared into the wind, asking if anybody had a light. We knew that one of the girls smoked, and that she had a lighter with her, but she didn't own up and we certainly weren't going to say anything. He said that he didn't think there would be another boat, so we would have to stay on the island. The plan was to make a human chain, and to go on our hands and knees up the cliff, but he had to have a light to lead us. Still, nobody said anything.

'For the hundredth time, Mr Cahillane asked him if the girls were safe on the mainland, and for the hundredth time the man assured the teachers that everyone was back safely in Dún an Óir. Mr Cahillane then promised us that no one would be punished for smoking if they produced a light. Miraculously, a lighter was handed up. We were linked together and ready to go up the cliff when we heard shouting and the roar of the outboard engine through the crashing of waves. Scared stiff, we had to make our way out along the slippery rocks again. The ferryman said that it was the last run, so some of us would have to stay. Like the captain of a stricken ship, Mr Cahillane said that the students should take the last boat home and the teachers would stay on the island. The ferryman shouted that four students would have to stay too. The volunteers were organised, me being one, while the teachers and the men continued their heated discussion. Then the plan was changed and he agreed to take all the students. When my turn came to jump, the fisherman tried to grab my kettle. I held on for dear life, despite being called every expletive under the sun. There was a bit of a tug of war, where he accused me of trying to drown everyone.

'All that I can recall of the trip back was being roared at to squash up together into the bow to keep the boat from flipping over. Waves slapped and soaked us from all angles and my hand bled from holding on. I think we were so scared, we didn't register the cold.

'Next thing we saw was the black outline of the cliffs above us. We could hear the surf thudding and crashing on the rocks, but couldn't see a thing. We weren't back at the pier at Dún Chaoin at all. We hadn't a clue where we were; all we knew was that we'd been dumped somewhere along the base of the cliffs at Dunmore Head. The reverse procedure happened. As the wave surged up the cliff face, we were hoisted up, one at a time, into the darkness, where invisible hands gripped and dragged us up the rock face, cutting and scratching us in the process. When I scrambled to my feet, I will never forget my shock at seeing eighty girls, clinging together on a shelf of rock, far below the cliffs, in the pitch darkness. I remember being utterly incredulous, not so much that we were being abandoned there, but by the fact that the ferrymen had told the teachers that everyone was in Dún an Óir. I knew that our teachers had agreed for us to be taken back only because of the assurance that we were being delivered safely to the bus driver and Sister Charles at Dún Chaoin. I was so angry. One of the ferrymen reassured us that we would be found soon. I wondered what he meant by "found." It obviously meant that nobody had a clue where we were.

'There was one diabetic girl who was ill at this stage. In the dark, I couldn't see how far below us the water was, but we were being drenched. I was afraid we'd be swept out to sea.

'I don't know how long it was we spent there, but it seemed like hours. Aileen and I were the farthest out from the base of the cliff, so we saw the lights first. A chain of about six lights jolted and swayed along the clifftop, like Christmas lights. We screamed and shouted, but they obviously didn't hear a thing over the roar of the waves and the wind. It was another age before the lights returned. This time they heard us, thank God, and we were hauled up the cliff, one by one, by men with ropes. Sister Carmel was crying when we met her. Two girls had stayed in the cottages with her because they were scared of boats. They said that they had ended up saying the Rosary all day and all night for us. They weren't convinced that it was we who had got the raw deal. Sister Charles had raised the alarm when we hadn't returned, and it was the fishermen and farmers drinking in Kruger's Pub who searched for us and found us.

'Sister Carmel had soup ready for us back at the cottages. We stayed awake all night, frozen through but, to be honest, I think it was more from shock than from cold. We were upset about the teachers, stuck in on the island, and I was so angry at how they had been deceived.

'We were supposed to have left for Waterford the previous evening, as far as I recall, so Sister Carmel had to ring the school and explain how we had lost three teachers!'

'I'm sure that caused consternation.'

'It did. Next morning, there was no let-up in the weather. The only difference from the previous evening was the fact that you could actually see the huge waves. If we had seen what we were getting into the night before, I think there would have been more than just teachers on a sleepover in Peig's house.'

'But did the teachers get back?' Sarah asked. 'What happened to them?'

'They did. A boat from Dingle went over for them later in the afternoon. I still remember Miss MacRoberts, her auburn curls wet and tangled, her clothes filthy and her eye make-up smudged. We were gobsmacked – Miss MacRoberts like we had never thought possible. Then Miss MacDonagh stepped up onto the pier, unfazed, beaming, like a Girl Guide, all set for her next adventure. In classes afterwards, we weaselled the details out of her. They had had to make their way up the island in the darkness with only the lighter to help them. Then the very ones who told me not to interfere with a kettle broke into Peig's house. Once inside, Miss MacDonagh tore up cardboard boxes and lit a fire with whatever she could find. She even burned some of Peig's old banisters.

'Back at school, we were comparing cuts and bruises for days. I had done particularly well on that front. My face, legs and arms were skinned, and I had a most impressive bandage on my hand.'

'I'm sure you milked it for as long as you could.'

'I did: my fifteen minutes of fame. We heard that the ferryman left Dún Chaoin shortly afterwards and went to England. On the day of our trip, his ferry was in Wales for maintenance work, so he decided to take us across in inflatable dinghies – those were the days when none of us had heard of Health and Safety Statements. So that's it – my school trip to the Great Blasket Island. I've often thought about it since, and wanted to see the place again . . . so here I am.'

'Have you still got the kettle?' Sarah asked.

'I have. It's at home by the fire in my study.'

'Why don't you bring it back here?'

'I suppose if I left it here now, some little vandal like I was would take it, or the yellow digger over there would bury it in the foundations of the new restaurant.'

'I can't believe they're allowed to go ahead with that. It will destroy the island. Surely people are opposed to it?'

'They are, but the problem is that many of the dwellings on the island were sold to an American about thirty years ago. Taylor Collings was a pilot from Alabama, with some idea for a holiday island. Ireland was a lot shorter of cash then, and most people sold him their holdings for a song. Subsequently, a local property developer bought up the houses from Collings and that's how all this came about.'

'It's the spirit of the island as it is that people come to experience. Development won't be long about ruining that,' Michael said.

'So will you never bring the kettle back then?' Sarah asked.

'I might. If it becomes a National Park, or maybe even a World Heritage Site, then the kettle comes back.'

'I think that's called blackmail,' Michael smiled.

'If that's what it takes. Kearney's kettle will only return to the island as it is.'

Happy Moonday

The next morning was the first time for weeks that Owen's boat had appeared on the sea. Owen, a brother of the twin ferrymen, advertised boat trips around the outer Blasket Islands, but his vessel had been in Dingle with engine trouble since my arrival. At last I would have a chance to visit An Téaracht, with its lighthouse and hundreds of puffins. I would see Inis na Bró, with its spectacular sea arch and cathedral rocks. And then Inis Mhic Uibhleain, with its magical fairy music and C. J. Haughey's herd of red deer. Maybe I would even persuade Owen to drop me off.

I raced down the path, sliding on the morning dew, to ask Sue to radio Owen to make sure that he would call into the island to pick me up. Next, I hurried back up to the hut, throwing binoculars, camera, bread, banana and water bottle into my bag. I slung it over my shoulder and pulled the door to, just as Michael hailed me from the lower path.

'Hello, Anita. By any chance has Sarah been with you this morning?'

'No. I haven't seen her.'

He looked down over the island, at a loss, flattening his hair, over and over again. 'I don't know what's got into her.

We're supposed to be getting the first ferry off the island today. She hasn't even packed, and she never came back for her breakfast. I can't find her anywhere.'

'Did you have a falling out?'

'No, not at all. She was upset last night, I suppose, at the idea of the end of the holiday. I won't see her until the Halloween break. She was off form and then just refused to talk to me, which is most unlike her. Now, she's disappeared. I've tried Seán and Laura, but they haven't seen her either. I don't know what to do.'

'It sounds as if she wants to be on her own for a while. Maybe you need to give her time, and she'll come back when she's ready. I'm sure nothing has happened.'

Michael did not look so sure. He paced, scanning the clifftops. Then he flopped down onto the grassy bank, holding his forehead in his hands.

'Just give me a few minutes,' I said. 'I'll tell Sue to be on the lookout.' I ran down the path at high speed for the second time that morning, bursting in Sue's door. 'Cancel Owen. I can't go, sorry.' After a few words in Irish over the radio, we watched the little boat change course, and disappear around the headland. Sue headed to check the slipway for Sarah as I climbed back up the hill to Michael.

'Michael, Sarah came for a short walk with me yesterday and the morning before. She may have gone to either place. I can't imagine that she would have walked to the back of the island on her own, do you?'

'No.'

'Well, let's start with those two places. You take one, and I'll take the other. Head up the south path, behind the weaver's to the point, up there. That's An Gob, where I took her whale-watching the other day. As you round the first turn, you'll see the Skelligs, two pyramid-shaped islands on the horizon. Once you spot them, you'll see huge white rocks immediately to your left. You'll have to climb down to them. She may be sitting in under one of them, in the sunshine. If not, just continue around to the crossroads and up to the fort. I'm sure she won't have gone any farther than that.'

'OK, I'll head off this minute. Where will you go?'

'The Gravel Strand and Seal Cove, and then I'll go to the fort by the north path. It will take me longer to get there, so if I don't appear, just head back by the north path and we'll meet up.'

'Right. Thank you. I'm sure she's fine, but I can't help being worried.'

'I know. Go on! See you later.'

I cut across the banks and through the ruins to the cliff overlooking the beach. There was no sign of Sarah. Just then Sigrid came by on the cliff path. She agreed to search the beach and the village. As I walked the cliffs, around to the Gravel Strand, the Beverley Sisters kept pace with me offshore. Three business-like cormorants flapped a dead straight line over the waves between us, in their usual hell-bent fashion. A skylark rose on spirals of song, piercing the morning air.

The dark north-facing cliffs of the Gravel Strand were blind to the early morning sunshine. They cast wedges of black shadow across the narrow inlet, varnishing the toes of their radiant south-facing sisters in oily damp shade. At one tiny place, the sunny cliff wall had managed to pull in her skirts far enough to reveal a bright bight of warm sunshine on the pebbles. In that white triangle of light huddled Sarah's small figure. I was halfway down the steep climb before I called out to her. She buried her face in her knees and did not respond. As I dropped noisily onto crunching pebbles, she still ignored me.

'Hi Sarah. Been for a swim yet?'

Without looking up, she shook her head, obviously crying.

'Mind if I squeeze into your sunshine?'

She moved to the side, making room for the two of us in the sunny patch.

'I think you're right. It's probably too chilly down here for a swim.' We sat for a while without speaking. I watched the black water swell and sink against sequinned rock walls. Sarah wept quietly. 'If you tell me, maybe I can help.' She shook her head and suddenly erupted into loud, helpless sobbing.

'You can't,' she cried. 'It won't . . . stop. It won't . . . go away and I . . . I can't tell Dad. I don't . . . know what . . . to do.'

'Can you tell me what won't stop, Sarah?' Through gasps and tears, Sarah told me what had happened.

'It came last night, but . . . it didn't go. I thought . . . you got . . . it for only a few hours, but it was still here . . . this morning. What will I do? It won't go away.' She was shocked, afraid and utterly confused. When I hugged her, congratulating her on being the luckiest twelve-year-old girl that I knew, she stopped crying and looked at me in indignation.

'I'm not lucky. It's horrible.'

'May I tell you why I think it's wonderful? Today, you have become a *woman*. It is a more important day than your twenty-first birthday. We should be having a party.'

She was not convinced. I rummaged in my backpack, taking out everything she would need for the next two or three days.

'Three days!' she sighed, defeated. After clarifying the practicalities of her new situation, she decided to go for a swim by herself.

'OK, while you're having a dip and dressing, I'll make our breakfast and then we'll find your dad.'

Ten minutes later, her footsteps trudged back through the gravel and she flopped down onto the warm pebbles, refreshed. 'Happy Moonday, Sarah,' I announced, presenting her with a banana sandwich.

'Thank you.' She looked at me curiously. She was halfway through the sandwich before she asked. 'Why did you say Happy Moonday?'

'Well, because with your first period, you have begun to live by the rhythm of the moon. You are now what is called a *we-moon*, a woman.'

'What's my period got to do with the moon?'

'Do you know how long it takes the moon to revolve around the earth?' I asked her.

'Twenty-eight days. We did that in Geography.'

'That's right, and how long does it take from one period to the next?'

'A month? Twenty-eight days?'

'Exactly, and what makes the tides go in and go out?

'The moon.'

'Yes. The moon is like a great big magnet, and its pull has a huge effect on every fluid on earth. It's the moon that makes the sap rise and fall in plants, so that there's a best time in the month to plant a seed and a best time to pick a fruit. Now, your body is made up of about seventy per cent water, so as well as affecting the tides and the sap, the moon has a huge effect on us women and our periods.'

'Nobody's ever told me that before.'

'Well, today people don't understand the importance of the moon as well as they did in ancient times. Long ago, people measured time according to the movement of the moon. Every month had twenty-eight days, and that was divided into four weeks of seven days, with every week beginning with Moonday.'

'Like Monday?'

'That's where it comes from. Today is the first Moonday of the month, and it's your very own Moonday. Congratulations. Here, have a scone'.

For the first time that morning, Sarah was smiling. She was either happier with her period or else she thought that I was a nutcase.

'Come on, let's draw your Moonday and then we really must find your father.'

We crunched up through the pebbles to the smooth, sandy entrance of the cave. I used a dried stem of oarweed as my chalk.

'Imagine that this big stone is the earth. It's like the centre of a giant wheel.' I drew twenty-eight spokes in the sand, radiating out from the rock. 'The moon is at the tip of the spokes, wheeling around the earth. Now, you sit on the earth and watch me. I'm the moon and I've got twenty-eight nights to get around you.'

She sat on the stone, laughing and drawing her feet in under her, to avoid tripping the moon.

'Every night when you look up at me, I'll be in a different place, so I'll look a different shape to you. Tonight I'm a new moon, at the beginning of my cycle. When you look for me, you won't see me, because the sun is on the same side, making me invisible for the first three nights.' I threw a towel over my face and stood in turn at the tip of the first three spokes. 'Night one invisible, night two invisible, night three invisible. This new moon time is when women traditionally got their period, like you have. It's also the time when sap is low in plants. Here I am, on night four, and you can just about see a narrow sliver of my beautiful moon face, and it gets bigger with each night, five and six, until it is a half-moon, on day seven. I'm called the waxing moon. Sap begins to rise in plants again and it's the best time for planting seeds. My moon face keeps getting bigger and bigger as I step from night to night, until, here, on night fourteen, I am a big bright full moon in the sky. Because of this full moon, energy is bursting in everything.'

As I leap around, whooping and waving my towel, with as much lunatic energy as I can muster, Sarah is laughing at last. 'The tides at this time are called spring tides, and they are huge. The sap is full in plants, so it's the time to pick the juiciest fruits and it's the time when the woman releases a ripe egg into her womb. Let's put a little white pebble at the full moon nights of fourteen, fifteen and sixteen. That represents the egg. These three days are the most fertile time for a woman to conceive a baby. Now if we have the egg fertilised . . . excuse me . . . while I demonstrate. Option one. Place a towel under my top . . . and hey presto . . . we'll have a bump and a baby in nine months. Option two, we do not have the egg fertilised, so we have no bump, and the woman and the moon continue on their journey together, to the next phase. After that busy, bursting, bright full moon, things are dying down again.'

I replaced the towel, on the side of my head, ready to inch it across my face. 'I'm called the waning moon now, where I'm darkening and shrinking smaller and smaller for the next seven nights, until you can see only half my moon face on day twenty-one. The sap is falling in plants. The tides are getting lazier, as they were back over there on day seven. They're not bothered to go in very far, or to go out very far. Energy is falling downwards, as the moon continues to wane.' I dropped to my knees, the towel hiding over half of my face as I as struggled from spoke to spoke like a dying soldier. Sarah continued to giggle on her earth rock. 'In women, the womb is no longer enriched. Its lining is shrinking and home, here at day one again, my moon face has disappeared and the woman bleeds with the new moon.' Demonstration completed, the dying soldier finally collapsed onto the sand, as Sarah continued to survey the twenty-eight nights around her.

'That's really cool. Is it true?'

'Of course, it is.' I said, pulling the towel off my face. 'Look at the high spring tide today. You've got your period. I've actually got mine too, and it can't be just a coincidence that every civilisation since ancient times, in different parts of the world, all came up with the same idea. Even in Gaelic, the words for menstruation, period, calendar and month are similar.'

'But why don't we have twenty-eight days in every month now. It's all mixed up.'

'I know. The Romans changed it to the calendar months that we use today, so the new moon and full moon now fall on different dates every month.'

Sarah stood on her stone, turning slowly as she counted out the phases of the moon.

'So in fourteen more days when the moon is full, I will release an egg.'

'That's what happens and that's why it's such a celebration.'

She jumped off the stone and counted her fourteen steps from new to full moon aloud.

'In other countries, you would be having a big party to celebrate. All of the women in the family – mother, grandmother, sisters and aunties – get together and you would have a cake and presents. It is the day you become a woman, so the whole family celebrates the potential for a new generation.'

'That's not fair. Why don't we have a party in Scotland?'

'Well, nobody's stopping you. In my school, when a girl in my class has her Moonday, I bring a big cake in to class and all the girls give her a tiny gift.'

'What? Are they not embarrassed?'

'Well, early in September, they are. They can't even say the word "period". It's called thingies, yokies, monthlies, jilly-jollies, the curse, and a hundred and one other names. But once the first girl has her party and they understand what I've shown you here, everyone is excited about it and no girl has ever wanted to miss out on her cake and presents.'

'My cousin always says she can't go swimming 'cos she has her *friend*,' Sarah said, drawing a full moon in the sand around the white pebble. 'What kind of presents do they get?'

'Well, my rule is that it has to fit in a matchbox, so they put in hairbands, flowers, coins, sweets, things like that, but I always tell them that their parents' gift need not fit into a matchbox.'

'Do you think that Dad knows I'm supposed to get a present when I become a woman?' she asked wistfully.

'Well, you're a mercenary little we-moon!'

She squealed as the towel landed on her head.

'I suppose you might have to explain it to him.'

'There's one thing that I don't understand.' She stopped her orbiting for a few seconds, trying to put it into words. 'If you're supposed to have your period with the new moon, and release an egg with the full moon, why is it that everybody doesn't have their period at the same time?'

'Because today, we're surrounded by artificial magnets and artificial light which interfere with the moon's effect on us. Your television, microwave, computer, radio and mobile phone – all those things have magnetic fields which affect you. Then women take medicines and the pill. There are lots of different reasons. Then if you're ill, your body might delay releasing an egg because it doesn't have any extra energy. If you live in a city, it's very difficult to be in harmony with the moon. You're walking over huge power cables, you're walking under them. You're surrounded.'

'We're leaving the island today. I'm going to ring Mum and tell her. Will I tell her we're supposed to have a party?'

'If you want a party, you tell her you only become a "we-moon" once. Now what about finding your poor Dad and telling him first? He should be on his way back from the fort at this stage.' Sarah stepped from moon to moon, one last time, counting out the days to her day fourteen, and then on to her next period.

'It's really cool, isn't it?'

'It is. Now come on. Your dad will be worried sick.'

As we climbed over the top of the cliff, we could see Michael striding back along the north path.

'There's Dad! I have to tell him he owes me a present.' This time she jumped out of the way, anticipating the flying towel.

'Go on. I'll see you later . . . and Happy Moonday.'

'Byee.' She scampered off, calling to Michael, who waved back vigorously, like an air traffic controller on the brow of the hill.

I abandoned the idea of any walk that day. I didn't want to miss Sarah and Michael leaving. I sat out with a book, chatting to Aisling and the curious tourists who passed by. It was four o'clock before Michael and Sarah appeared, on their way to the ferry. I made tea, and we sat on the grassy bank talking, as two ferries came and went. Eventually, the red ferry moored in under the cliff for its last trip.

'Will you be here next year?' Sarah asked.

'You never know. I might be.' I hadn't thought any more than a day ahead for a long time, so the question baffled me.

Despite the warm sunshine, Sarah had one of Sue's beautiful purple and blue scarves wrapped around her shoulders, which she continually adjusted to her best advantage. Michael smiled at me.

'Her Moonday present. Thank you.'

Sarah then pulled a small brown bag from inside her sleeping bag roll.

'Happy Moonday to you too,' she said, presenting me with the package. Inside was one of Páid's wooden candle-holders.

As I hugged her, I felt my throat swell, taut as a drum. I didn't speak. She kissed me on the cheek and took off down the hill. 'Byee.'

'Looks like it's time to pick up that drama script again,' Michael laughed. He took my hand. 'Goodbye. And I can't thank you enough,' he said. He still held my hand, smiling awkwardly. 'And be more assertive with those donkeys.' I nodded, swallowing hard to quell waves of emotion. 'We'll definitely be back next summer,' he said finally.

I never managed to say goodbye. He smiled and released my hand.

He waved one last time from the clifftop, before disappearing down the slipway. I watched until the ferry disappeared into the shadow of the mainland. Then I went into the hut, closed the door and cried. The tears were new and warm. They spilled from a living spring, so different to the dead stagnant waters of earlier days. I thought again of the two little girls I had seen at the old National School and knew that, like them, I wouldn't meet Michael and Sarah again.

That night after dark, I began to write. I lit a candle, wrapped my sheepskin around me and poured my thoughts and dreams onto the page. At 3 a.m. I was finished. Until I left the island, I continued the same nightly ritual – story after story, in an effort to tell the story that couldn't be told.

Haughey's Isle

Throughout that month of August, the weather remained warm and calm. The ferries buzzed back and forth with cosmopolitan cargoes. The midges were out in force, flushing squealing lovers out of the undergrowth. One female camper ran to the ferry screaming that she was being eaten alive. She left her tent and belongings to be collected by the ferryman days later. Filling the vacuum after the departure of Michael and Sarah, I busied myself with excursions to the back of the island, bare feet in the damp turf and face into the sea breeze.

As I soaked in the sun, in the shelter of the Bright Dwellings at the far end of the Great Blasket Island, I frequently saw the tiny, lone figure walk from the direction of the stone house on Inis Mhic Uibhleain up to the huge rocks in the centre of the island. I always wondered if it was Charlie Haughey, and I became determined to take that trip to the outer islands, to find out.

One evening in return for giving a tour of the Blasket village to the crew of a passing yacht, they presented me with the opportunity.

'Do you fancy sailing around the islands tomorrow?'

I jumped at the chance. The following morning as we passed Inis Mhic Uibhleain, I could see the landing place. I wondered about going ashore. The skipper agreed with me. There was no harm in taking a few photos of red deer. Without giving it a second thought, I scrambled onto the rocks and climbed up the landing steps. Our approach to the island had obviously been under observation as a familiar male figure was waiting for me as I arrived at the top.

'How can I help you?' Charles J. Haughey asked me.

I was so surprised and breathless it took a while to explain the purpose of my visit. He listened and confirmed to me that he was that tiny figure I had seen.

'I regularly climb up to study the remains of the past. These stones have seen it all. Sometimes I feel like shaking the secrets out of them. Maybe some day archaeologists will develop a technology that will enable them to unveil the past more meaningfully, but in the meantime we can only gaze and wonder.'

I knew what he meant. Compared to the permanence and power of these islands, we are nothing, as insignificant as blown dust.

'Over there is what appears to be an ancient burial ground,' he said. He was silent for a time. 'I believe the oratory here, and the graves in front of it, are closely related to the monastic site on the Greater Skellig – probably some monks of the same order. Have you been to the Skelligs?'

'I have. I don't think I'll be invited back though. It's a long story. Perhaps the Blasket dwellings were actually part of the Skellig community?'

'Well, only the stones know at this stage,' he smiled. 'You know, I would have liked to have been an archaeologist.' We sat quietly for a time. Around us the remains of the oratory, beehive huts and old boundary walls lay silent. Only the sea breeze rustled through the grass. I thought of the yellow digger, gouging out layers of time back on the Great Blasket Island. At least here, in on the Inis, under its present caretaker, the secrets of the stones would remain intact.

'We've started an island log,' he said.

I understood his reasons. Recording the transitory comings and goings of migrating birds, visitors, winter gales, boats and grandchildren seemed to give an anchor in time, to validate us, before we became more flotsam on the tide.

'I always wanted to live on an island off the west coast of Ireland,' he added.

'Are you from the west?' I was only aware of the former Taoiseach in a Dublin context.

'I was born in Mayo,' he proclaimed with pride, planting his hands firmly on his knees. 'There's a place in Donegal called Haughey's Isle. I looked at it, but it is no longer an island, though it may have been at one time. Most of the islands off the west coast don't have any proper title, so I was at a dead end. Then Maria Simonds-Gooding suggested Inis Mhic Uibhleain.'

As Charlie talked about the Inis, he said, 'It is known as the island of the fairies – *na púcaí*, where they play fairy music, to carry away the very soul. On a summer's evening, at twilight, when the sea murmurs below, and the haunting cry of the seals echoes in the caves, it's relatively easy to believe anything.'

I knew that this man felt the spirit of the islands. I told him of my experience with the two little girls at the old schoolhouse.

'I have never seen anything on the Inis myself, but Maria had a terrifying ghostly experience here. It was while she was in here on one of those painting visits, in the early days, that she saw the ghost.'

Curious, I asked him to tell me about it, but he just smiled. 'You'll just have to talk to Maria about that. That is *her* story to tell. Tom and Paddy Ó Dálaigh owned the island at that time. They were bachelor brothers, and kept sheep on the island. As long as they lived, we gave them the grazing for their sheep. When they were in clipping the sheep, they stayed in that *bothán* over there.'

'How long ago was that?'

'It was in the seventies. We're here over thirty years now. It was a great place for the children to holiday, and learn about the sea, and develop respect for it. They were out boating, swimming, exploring and climbing from one end of the day to the other, and now the grandchildren can have that same freedom. We had to build up the landing place – *an leirigh*. That was, and still is, probably, the most forbidding aspect of island life, trying to land. You waited for the boat to rise on the swell and jumped, hoping for the best. The climb up from the sea to here is heavy-going, just as bad as the harbour in Dún Chaoin.'

Memories of our school trip where we jumped into the rocky darkness from the rising waves came flooding back. I recounted our disastrous landing on the cliffs below Dunmore Head back in 1979.

'I heard about that,' he said. 'It's gone down in the Kerry annals, a bit like the wine story.'

I was at a loss. 'What's the wine story?'

He looked at me in disbelief. 'It is a Blasket story that has become folklore by now. You must have heard it.'

I waited in anticipation. A cloud formation rested on the western horizon, like a distant island.

'We tell the grandchildren that is Hybrasil, and that we had tried sailing out west, looking for it, but never found it.' He gazed out to sea and recited:

'On the ocean that hollows the rocks where ye dwell.
A shadowy land has appeared, as they tell.
Men thought it a region of sunshine and rest
And they called it Hybrasil, the Isle of the Blessed.'

I thought of Fergal's boat, *Oileán na nÓg*, called after the mythical island where nobody ever grows old. Myth and history, always, seemed to be a vital part of our present, on these mystical islands.

A deer stag inched his way towards us, nuzzling and chomping the grass on the clifftop. We watched him silently. Behind him the infinite expanse of blue sky merged into three thousand miles of Atlantic Ocean.

'Why did you bring the deer into the island? Would introducing a new species not change the natural balance here?'

'No, not at all. There were always sheep here, and the red deer and sheep are very similar in their behaviour and in what they eat. The red deer were very natural successors to the sheep, particularly since there are no trees on the Inis. The red deer is a native species that has survived in Ireland since the last Ice Age. When I came to the island, the only native herd in the country was in Killarney. At that time, that herd was under threat and falling in numbers. Any major setback, like foot and mouth disease, would mean that unique genetic link with the past would be gone forever.'

'There are red deer in Wicklow and Donegal.'

Yes, there are and they are a very important part of our wildlife heritage, but they are not the native pure-bred Irish red deer. They were brought in from Scotland and England in the nineteenth century. The Killarney herd was then the only native herd of red deer, the same deer that the Fianna hunted. Inis Mhic Uibhleain provided a unique opportunity

Red deer on Inis Mhic Uibhleain.

to preserve the native species. It gave us the base on which to build up a reserve herd, so that if the Killarney herd was ever threatened again, it could always be renewed from here. The Inis turned out to be an ideal habitat for the deer. They thrived and there are now over a hundred. We brought in the native Irish hare, another link in our wildlife heritage chain, and they are doing very well too.'

There it was, that word 'heritage,' again. 'It's a pity that heritage isn't a priority in Ireland today,' I said.

'*Heritage*. They can't even spell the word.'

I watched the regal stag lift his head, smelling the wind. Behind him, An Téaracht rose from the sea like a volcano. Its pinnacle was topped with a motionless hazy cloud. The stag bolted and disappeared down the hillside. 'I almost expected to see Fionn and Oisín in hot pursuit there.'

Charlie smiled. 'I am afraid I cannot arrange that, but at home in Dublin, we have Cú Chulainn.' I had heard of it. 'It is a larger-than-life statue, carved by Joan Walsh Smith from the trunk of a fallen elm. We lost some elms in a gale in the early eighties. Joan carved Cú Chulainn out of one of them, and he now stands patiently on guard outside Abbeville.'

'Well if Oisín came across the sea again, he would feel quite at home here, even now,' I said, watching the larks spiralling up from the springy grass around the walls of the oratory.

'Yes, I suppose it hasn't really changed.'

His gaze then fell upon the house. 'Well, the rate of wine consumption and the solar panels might *throw him*, just a bit.' He chuckled to himself. I was slow to pick up his joke. 'I don't think Oisín needed solar energy to power his mobile phone.'

'You still have to tell me the wine story,' I reminded him.

He looked at me and said 'my version . . . and I don't

want to be quoted.' I sat back in delight while he regaled me with a tale of French wine, storm-bound builders, and French presidents. 'Now, you will have to go to Larry Slattery over in Dún Chaoin to hear the full story of that episode, over a pint.'

'You mean the ferrymen's father?'

'The very same gangster,' he said affectionately.

The yacht returned for me much too quickly. Charlie walked to the top of the cliff with me when I was leaving. 'Come back and see me again soon. You can tell me your Skellig story next time. I love to hear about the islands.'

We shook hands and said goodbye. I set off down the steep path. As I looked back up, he waved. Behind him, a herd of red deer grazed by the ruins of the ancient oratory. As I waved back, I knew that the secrets of the stones on this particular Blasket Island were in safe hands.

Blasket Wine

L arry Slattery arrived into the Great Blasket Island a few days later. He was a jovial man who had time to chat with everyone. I approached him, as he stood on the cliff, above the slipway, watching the red ferry depart. He pushed the cap back off his head, wiping the sweat from his brow.

'Charlie told you to ask me,' he said and burst into guffaws of laughter. 'That's a good one. What did he say about it?'

'Well, he laughed a fair bit too.'

'The man has a sense of humour, I'll say that for him, and it was lucky for us that he does.'

'What happened?'

'You know he built a house in on the Inis?' I nodded. 'Well, I was in helping Dan, when we did the deed.'

'Who's Dan?'

'Dan Brick. *Brick*, the builder!' he grinned. 'When he started building first, there was only a tiny builder's prefab there, for shelter and for making tea. It was fairly primitive. Most people imagine C. J. H. in a Caribbean paradise, but I can tell you, in on the Inis it was rough – no electricity, running water, firewood or toilet. When the wind and rain beat across the island, no work could be done of course. It was slow going. Loading and unloading materials, and even getting to the site left you at the mercy of the weather. Sure, you'd be exhausted before you'd even start.

'At one stage, the weather turned really vicious. There was Dan, myself and two other lads stranded in on the island for a few weeks. Our supplies were soon gone, so what could we do only investigate Charlie's stores. Luckily for us, his kids had an amount of tins of food put by, for when they might be caught out. We did OK for a while on tins of ham, but I had to draw the line at tins of snails. French snails, if you don't mind. I even had a go at making a kind of bread over the open fire. We were getting pretty hungry, I can tell you.

'Anyway, Dan sent me off to see what else I could find, and there it was – a case of wine. The boss told me to get a bottle and we'd try it. He said he didn't think Charlie would mind. I poured it out, into the two old tin mugs that the Ó Dálaigh brothers used for the tea.' He cringed as he remembered. 'It was very rare French wine that he had been given as a gift. He had been nursing it for years, waiting for a special occasion. Nineteen forty-seven was on that bottle. It could have been the year they built the wine factory for all we knew. I suppose if we'd known how much each swig of the stuff was worth, we might have sipped it a bit more slowly, but to be honest, I didn't taste much in it.'

'Was it the most expensive bottle you drank?'

'Bottle! Are you joking? We drank the whole case.'

'Châteauneuf-du-Pape nineteen thirty-five was on the second bottle. According to Charlie, you can't put a value on wine like that. Thank God he has a sense of humour. He seemed to get a great laugh out of the fact that we downed it out of the two ancient chipped, tin mugs of the Ó Dálaigh's.

We were stranded out there another two weeks after that. Now that I think of it, there was a bottle of vodka that we drank too. I'd forgotten about that. There was no sign of anyone coming out for us, so the four of us set off across the nine miles in a currach, and do you know, we did it in three hours,' he announced proudly. 'Three hours non-stop rowing to Dún Chaoin. Not bad going, eh?'

'But what about the wine? Were you not afraid that Charlie would miss it?'

'Sure Dan said we'd buy a couple of bottles in Garvey's supermarket in Dingle, and Charlie would be none the wiser.'

'That obviously didn't happen.'

'No, not quite. A couple of months later, Charlie came into the island with the architect and a few others, to see how the work was progressing. It was sweltering hot weather. He spotted me sitting on box outside the *bothán*, and over he came for a word. We were chatting about this and that, when, didn't he decide that we both needed a drink! I offered him a cup of tea but he looked at me as if I was half-mad. Then, he proceeded to tell me where his treasured case of wine was stashed! This was the celebration he had waited years for, and he was going to open a very special bottle. I was nearly sick. I suppose I should have been honoured that it was me he thought of drinking it with, and not the hobnobs he'd come over with. I couldn't get away fast enough, but sure there was nothing I could do. I arrived back with the two tin mugs and a bottle of plonk with one of those screw-on caps, which we'd bought in Garvey's. He assumed that I couldn't find the wine and he said he'd get it, so what could I do but look the man in the eye, and tell him that we'd drunk it.'

'What did he say?'

'Well, I had to assure him a fair few times that we had, in all honesty, drunk the entire case. He was like somebody that was been told that one of the family had died, and it just wasn't sinking in. I thought it was the end of me. Then would you believe it, he just put his head in his hands, and he laughed and laughed. He wanted to know all the details. He seemed to get great good out of the idea of the whole case being downed in the old tin mugs, like tea. He was breaking his sides laughing. I was in a bit of a state over it, so I reassured him that we had replaced the wine with much newer stuff from the supermarket.'

'What did he say then?'

'Nothing, he just didn't stop laughing, and then he nearly cracked up altogether when he saw that the £1.50 price tag was still on it. Anyway, when he eventually drew breath, he sent me off to retrieve the empty bottles and corks. Then I got my first lesson on wine, as we sat on the old box in the sunshine. All I know about wine Charlie Haughey has taught me, and since then, I have a healthy respect for the grape. If there's any trace of it still in my bloodstream, I'm worth a fortune.'

I didn't know anything about fine wines, but even I could appreciate the travesty of a treasured case of rare wine meeting its end, swilled down in a chipped tin mug with nothing but a tin of ham for company.

'You know that story has gone around the world like a boomerang. Charlie told it to President Mitterrand at a state dinner the following weekend, and it was told back to him in the States a couple of weeks after that.

'When the house was finished, he invited me, along with half the population of Dingle and Dún Chaoin, into the Inis, for the party. He's like that you know . . . but let me tell you, I brought a bottle with a real cork that time.'

The Black Calf

According to Larry, Maria Simonds-Gooding would be in to visit the island the following morning. I watched the ferry arrivals carefully. I looked out for an easel or other such give-away. There was none. A homogenised crowd seeped through the lower ruins. Then a tall striking lady set off alone, up to the top of the hill. She radiated an enthusiasm and energy that set her apart. Near the brow of the hill she stopped, framing vast views with her hands. Like a fairy godmother, with one wave of her magic brush, she could immortalise all before her. That had to be her. I locked the door and set off in hot pursuit.

When I greeted her, she turned, smiling broadly, and introduced herself as Maria Simonds-Gooding. After chatting for a while, I asked her if she would tell me her ghost story of the Inis.

'My goodness, I'm surprised you've heard about that. Not many people know about the calf on the Inis. It was a long time ago, but I remember it clearly, every bit of it. It was July 1968 and was one of the hottest summers I can remember. There wasn't a breath of wind. I wanted to get out, onto one of the islands, to do some painting. One day, in Kruger's pub,

I met the skin-divers who were searching for the Spanish Armada shipwreck. They promised to take me out to whatever island I wanted. I organised my things and met them, as arranged, down at the Cusheen, at three o'clock. I had a sack with food and a bottle of Kruger's port. My cousin Marie-Claire was with me. We decided on Inis Mhic Uibhleain, but the problem was how to land. The wreck of a small German plane was visible as we approached the pebble beach, on the east side of the island. We made several unsuccessful attempts to land, until eventually we took the dinghy in and managed to tie it to a rock while we climbed the steep cliff onto the island. My sack was hauled up the rocks on the end of a rope.'

Maria paused as she closed her eyes, remembering. 'You know, I can still smell that port. The bottle had smashed and it had soaked into everything. The skin-divers left us alone on the island, saying they would come back for us in a week. We walked the island and decided to put up our tent in the field that was walled in for a blind sheep. It had been another very hot day and now it was an utterly still night. It was difficult to sleep, with the heat, and the noise of all the birds.

'It was on the third night that it happened. We had the weeniest of tents and I remember that I had three beetles in my sleeping bag that night. At eleven o'clock every night, like clockwork, the storm petrels came in from the sea. The noise was deafening. The storm petrels were all flying in from as far as forty miles away, back to their nests in the stone walls around the field. They were everywhere. Then there were the chilling wails of the manx shearwater. There was no hope of any sleep. We had to shout at each other to be heard over the racket. We had a plan to divert them, so we got up and lit the lantern.

'Marie-Claire set off with the lantern, down to the end of the field, in the hope that the birds would be attracted to the light. I stood by the tent watching. She was walking with all these birds and bats flying around. Suddenly, the next thing I saw and heard was a black calf, pounding down the field behind her. He was pounding, rather than running, and with great force, as though he was driving her on.'

Maria crossed her arms protectively, in front of her, as she took a deep breath and continued. 'I roared and roared and roared at her. I roared so much, I was hoarse for days. The calf had a driving force that caused absolute terror in me. Marie-Claire came rushing back. She was quite cross with me and wanted to know what I was shouting at. I couldn't believe it. She hadn't seen a thing – nothing. How she failed to hear the calf behind her, I really couldn't understand.

'I was shocked and upset, but I'm not one to give up. I got over it, and a week later, after the skin-divers had come in and collected Marie-Claire, I remained on the island alone. They promised to come back for me in a few weeks, weather permitting.'

'Did she leave because of what had happened?'

'No, nothing to do with that. She was only just married, and was keen to be with her husband – that was always the plan. I never saw the calf again, although I stayed on another couple of weeks.

'After I returned to the mainland with the skin-divers, things began to happen very quickly. Within three weeks, I had bought the cottage that I now live in, in Dún Chaoin. It was the nearest thing to living on the Great Blasket. An islander who left the island before the evacuation in 1953 owned it. He had nothing when he came across. He even brought the roof off his island house and put it on the cottage. It had no electricity or running water. He then moved to Dingle with his sister.

'Lisa Mitchell was my neighbour. She's dead now, God rest her. Her people were from the Inis. "Do you know the story of the calf?" She asked me this as we sat by her fire. I was shocked, because I had not told her about my experience. She told me the following: "a black calf appeared on the Inis, it came into Tigh na hInise. Nobody had any idea where it had come from, or how it could possibly have got there. At that time, there were only four cows and four calves on the island. There are two versions of the story. One is that they took the calf in and gave it milk. The other is that they did not give it milk. Whichever way it was, the calf walked down the island with the four calves and cows after it, and they all followed it straight over the cliff to their deaths."

'That was no ordinary calf – of that I am sure.'

I was baffled. It was such a bizarre story. I could understand the relevance of my ghostly encounter on the Great Blasket Island, but Maria's experience with the black calf was inexplicable. We wondered at the thin veil between worlds as we shared stories.

Naturally she wondered how I had heard about her and the black calf. Once I admitted that it had been Charlie Haughey who had set me on her trail, she insisted that I tell her my Skellig story before I had a chance to tell him.

'Fair trade,' I agreed.

Skellig Reunion

The road to the top of Sceilg Mhichíl was paved with many steps . . . 206, 207, 208 . . . I thought I was going to have a heart attack . . . 209, 210 . . . according to Des Lavelle's *Skeillig Story: Ancient Monastic Outpost*, there are at least 500 steps . . . 211, 212 . . . a group of young French students filed past me . . . 213, 214 . . . One boy was dizzy from the height, but they still did not slacken their pace. They formed a human chain and he was swept along . . . 215, 216 . . . A German couple bounded ahead of me like two spring lambs. If it weren't for pride, I would have crawled on my hands and knees . . . 217, 218 . . . The first time I had been on Sceilg Mhichíl, I had been ten years younger, and I had met only the two resident lighthouse keepers . . . 219 . . . The second time, I carried a decade of arthritic rust and seemed to have met the Berlin Busman's Holiday . . . 220.

Still, pride comes before a fall. I decided to take a break. I flopped onto a step, gulping down my water. Was 220 the one I was sitting on or the one my feet were on? Each step was at least a metre across and 15 centimetres deep. How a cold, hungry monk could have hand-carved each stone, over 1,500 years ago, I could not fathom. Either he was sent out there for penance, cursing like a trooper, or he did it as a misguided act of love for us future pilgrims. He could never, however, have envisaged that pilgrim trail of American baseball caps and Japanese cameras that would follow in his wake.

At last two locals approached. 'Me legs just isn't able,' the old man panted as he stopped, head bowed, below me. He did not move for some time. Páid was seventy-five and from Ventry. Kathleen, his sister, was overweight and under severe pressure.

'Páid, we'll miss the boat if we don't start back down. Come on let you!'

Immediately, the frail man set off, climbing painfully upwards again. He was very unsteady.

'You go on down. I'll be grand.' He stooped forward, lifting one leg up onto the next step. Then he rested, leaning both hands on that knee, before dragging up the other leg. The old man seemed oblivious to the 150-metre drop to his right, as tourists swept past him, on the left. It was clear that he was not going to take a blind bit of notice of anything that Kathleen might say.

'Stubborn old fool' were her parting words, as she began sidestepping heavily back down. Páid was anything but that. Amid the trail of hiking boots, trendy fleece jackets and zoom lenses, Páid's old-fashioned wool suit and cap battled courageously on.

I introduced myself, assuring him that I was as tired as he was, which was not far from the truth. During his next ten painful steps, we had to sit twice. As he laboured to catch his breath, I chatted about my first visit to the Skelligs back in 1986. Only the lighthouse keepers were on the rock then. Mick Fitzpatrick had given me a tour around his rock. He was passionate about the monastic site, the sea and the solitude. He was enthralled, protective and reverent towards the place. I told Páid that it had been one of the most special places I had ever been.

'We said that too. It is forty-four years since we were here. That was back in 1954. Mary and I were married that week.' He was quiet with his memories for a time and then continued. 'We had two nights in Killarney, and then a friend of the cousin took us out to Sceilg Mhichíl. In them days, I was up to the top like a goat, and Mary was as quick. There was no such thing as visitors on the island back then, just Mary and me, on the top of the world till evening. We had the best of times.' Seeing his rheumy eyes glisten, I knew that was true. 'We always said we'd come back, but sure, then the boys were born and the years just disappeared on us.'

As he fell silent, we watched the tiny ferries bobbing like toys over 150 metres below. They disgorged their passengers and waves of coloured fleeces flowed by us. Páid made no move to get up.

'How many children have you?' I asked.

'We've three boys. John and Pat are married in Boston, and Stephen is working on the buildings in London.' As he brushed the cap back off his face, I could see the beads of sweat shining on his forehead. 'It's just meself now. Mary passed on in April.' He looked as if he would continue, but no words came out. I looked away, pretending to make out Pat Murphy's boat in the flotilla. I made some clichéd comment about the comfort of having three wonderful sons, as I watched microscopic kittiwakes criss-crossing over the silken waves below us.

'Well, to give her her due, she never missed a Sunday writing to them. Had to be Sunday. She'd get three parish newsletters after mass, and each one was wrapped up tight as a rolling pin in *The Kerryman*, and then it was off to the post office on the Monday morning. Even after the radiotherapy, she kept wrapping up those parcels.'

After a few moments, he struggled to his feet with renewed determination. I was terrified that he would stumble over the edge; one gust of wind would have carried him off the rock. I held him gently by the elbow.

'Páid, the view is beautiful from here. Would you not like to sit here, and I'll go ahead, and take a photo for you at the top?' For another three steps, he struggled on. Maybe he had not heard me.

Suddenly he collapsed onto his hands and knees. 'Me legs just isn't able,' he panted. He kept repeating it in frustration. I sat down beside him, feeling at a total loss.

'I'll go back down with you, Páid. It'll be like the January sales at the top with that lot.' He sat on the step, leaning his elbows on his knees, bony wrists and hands cradling his forehead. It took all his willpower to catch his breath.

'This is the last time I'll be on the Skellig. I have to leave something back on the top of the rock while I'm here. I promised Mary I'd do it.'

'Could I do it for you, Páid?' I asked him.

He took something from his coat pocket. It was an old white linen handkerchief, wrapped carefully around two pieces of white quartz. Originally they had been one piece. He slotted them together perfectly, holding them so tightly, that his knuckles went white. Then, without a word, he rewrapped them in the handkerchief, and hurriedly placed the parcel in my hands.

'Promise me you'll put them back together in the shrine, under the high cross.' I knew exactly where he meant.

'I promise. I know the quartz mound. It's right next to the oratory.'

He nodded. 'You'll be sure to put them there?'

'Páid, on my life, I promise. I'll put them there, and I'll say a prayer for you and Mary. You start making your way down slowly, and I'll meet you below, and tell you when I have it done.'

He said nothing, just cupped his hand over mine.

My last image of Páid was of his frail thin back, bent over the steep steps of Sceilg Mhichíl. I placed the quartz in my small backpack and set off with renewed determination. I imagined the moment that I would tell him the twin stones were safely installed. I would take a photo for him too, as proof.

I began overtaking people, anxious to get to the top and back down before Páid left. I forced my screaming knees up the last 300 steps without resting. Close to the top, I had to stop. There was a queue of people, headed by a huge crowd, near where I remembered the entrance should have been. It seemed an eternity before I was anywhere near the front. I kept looking at my watch, trying to gauge Páid's progress down.

A young guide, with reflective blue sunglasses, recited the Skellig pamphlet, with as much speed as a corpse at a christening. At this rate, I knew that I'd never make it back down for Pat Murphy's last boat, never mind Páid's. After shuffling from foot to foot for another ten minutes, I boldly left the crowd of tourists, heading for the stone tunnel that led into the monastic site.

'Excuse me, madam. Get back in line and wait your turn.' I blushed to the tips of my earlobes, under the censure of twenty German frowns and the blue reflective shades. I attempted to say something about not needing the tour, just having a message to drop off. 'Get down, madam!' The guide ignored what I had said. I stood at the wall like a bold child. There were wire barriers everywhere. Workmen in yellow and blue hats wandered by.

'Ladies and gentlemen, a helicopter is coming in. Please stay where you are and cover your eyes!'

A blonde female guide herded a group out through the tunnel, as the noise of the chopper got louder. Suddenly it appeared over the edge of the rock, a line suspended from its belly, trailing a sling of concrete cargo. The grit swirled, the pebbles scattered, and the blades roared.

'Now, ladies and gentlemen, you may re-enter for five minutes for photographs,' she announced. I was getting desperate. It seemed an age before they emerged.

Blue Shades spoke. 'Ladies and gentlemen, you may now enter. Sit on the two ledges. You may not wander around the cells during the lecture. You will be given some time for photographs later.'

I felt none of the wonder and reverence I had felt with the lighthouse keeper ten years before. The yellow Men At Work signs and red Danger signs were everywhere. A mobile phone suddenly rang from inside Cell B. *Cells A, B and C*! The lighthouse keepers had had a saint's name for every cell, and a story to go with it. Blue Shades had the dimensions and statistics. We sat obediently on the two ledges and listened to his recitation. His mobile phone rang.

'Ladies and gentlemen, you must leave immediately. Back out through the tunnel quickly! The helicopter is coming in for another drop.'

I looked over to the standing stone cross, outside the oratory. The bed of quartz was at its foot, exactly as Páid had described. Between my destination and me flashed the trendy sunglasses. All I could see was my reflection clutching the handkerchief. 'May I just drop this here before –'

'You heard me, madam. Leave the area!'

The sound of the helicopter approached. Day-Glo jackets and cameras jostled through the tunnel. I had no option. I followed at the rear under the glare of the blue shades. Outside the grit swirled, the crowd huddled into itself, and my eyes streamed. It was more like a scene from wartime Vietnam than from a peaceful monastic settlement.

'Now, ladies and gentlemen, would the next group please enter the site?'

'Vot about our votografen?' one of the Germans in my group protested.

'Sorry, sir, you had your time inside. It's another group's turn now.'

The next group began to file in, as my group was ushered brusquely back towards the steps. The guide guarded the entrance but I managed to duck in. I dodged behind an Italian couple. The new group was settling obediently on the ledge. I darted over towards the quartz shrine. Before I was 3 metres from the shrine he was on to me. 'No wandering around during my talk. You'll have plenty of time to take photos later,' he announced at the top of his voice to the group, as he barred my way.

'Excuse me.' I was definitely going to miss Páid. 'I've actually heard the talk, I just need to –'

'Madam, sit down!' Taken aback, I turned away from my reflection and sat on the ledge. I was distraught at this stage. Páid would be gone. He would never know that I had returned the honeymoon stones but, worse than that, I was beginning to think I would not manage to return them at all. The guide and his blonde companion had me under surveillance. They would have me up for interfering with a National Monument next. His talk seemed to take an eternity again.

'Now, ladies and gentlemen, you have five minutes to take some photographs. Stay in the designated area. You may not go up behind the cells where the ground is loose.'

Twenty people scattered amongst the beehive huts with their cameras. I escaped into the darkness of the first beehive hut that I came to. I flopped onto the ground, leaning back against the coolness of stone. For the first time, I was alone and relief surged through my whole body. As my eyes adjusted to the dim light, I gradually made out the 1,500-year-old corbelled roof. I was transported back to the awe of that first day on the Sceilg Mhichíl with the lighthouse keeper.

'The spirit of the rock soothes the soul,' Mick Fitzpatrick had said. He often requested to stay for a second and third continuous term of duty on the light. I stroked the worn stone, invoking hundreds of years of prayer and peace.

'Tom, where's the other fucking sack?' barked a workman outside, as his feet tramped along the back of the monk's cell, which was at my head height. Suddenly the guide's denim legs cut off the shaft of sunlight that had been streaming through the low doorway.

'Ladies and gentlemen, please leave the enclosure immediately. The helicopter is coming in.' I would have come out with my hands up, but all sense of humour had failed me. I had failed Páid.

Blue Shades escorted me to the tunnel, while ignoring the rest of the group. Outside the grit swirled and settled, and the helicopter left once more. 'Now, ladies and gentlemen, return down to the cove. Next group, enter please.' I didn't move. I stood humiliated and defeated. He repeated his instructions – for my benefit, I am sure. As I turned away, only anger stopped my tears.

I thanked God that Páid hadn't made it to the top. The mystical and romantic monastic site, which Páid and Mary had treasured, was gone. Nothing remained but a circus, a building site, and a curiosity for tourists and archaeologists alike. It had become something to tick off on a must-see list, 'Skelligs – been there, done that.'

It was 1.45 p.m. Páid's boat would have departed fifteen minutes earlier. I left the site. My chest was a knot of anger and disappointment. A narrow peaty path ascended at an angle from the main track. I stepped up onto it, away from the crowd, scrambling up onto the flat rock. I was higher than anybody on the island. On one side of the island, the boats rocked on the dazzling blue; on the other side, white surf crashed against rocks, over 200 metres below me. I sat on the flat rock, shaking with frustration.

Then, everything happened so suddenly. The helicopter approached. The guides and tourists left the site quickly. Everybody covered their eyes, sheltering against walls or shoulders. The top of the rock became a swirling, choking roar of dust. As everybody shrank from the scene, I leaped up, clambering blindly up the bank and over the wall. I found myself behind the top beehive hut. The helicopter roared in my ears. My eyes stung and my hair and clothes whipped around me. An image of soldiers going over the top in the First World War flashed through my mind, as my heart pounded. I was stung all over by flying gravel and debris. Expecting to be fired on, by the chopper or a sniper in reflective sunglasses, I dodged and dived as fast as I could to the target. Crouching at the foot of the quartz shrine, with my eyes tightly shut, I fumbled for the handkerchief in my backpack. Blindly, I unwrapped the two quartz stones, reconnecting them tightly, directly under the high cross. Páid and Mary had their honeymoon stones restored and reunited at last.

I felt invincible. Stone me or shoot me, I did not care. My mission was accomplished. I stood by the high cross, alone, as the roar of the chopper blades receded and the dust began to settle again. I said a silent prayer for Páid and Mary at the foot of the quartz shrine. Touching the high cross, I took a treasured look around the deserted oratory and beehive huts that survived, perched on the edge of the world. An Sceilg Bheag was a lonely, inhospitable neighbour in the sparkling sapphire sea below. It rose like a small alp, covered in brilliant white guano, making a spectacular backdrop to the high cross. For the first time that day, I was filled with the cries of thousands of nesting sea birds. I reached for the sky, like many had done there before me, and then I slipped out through the stone tunnel before the noise of the next group could break the spell.

As I emerged, I came face to face with my smile, reflected in the blue shades. 'Goodbye,' I called cheerily, as I waved Páid's handkerchief above me, in the blue sky.

I never did see Páid again to tell him that I had replaced their love stones. Pat Murphy and the other ferrymen did not notice a frail old man in a dark wool suit. I did not know his surname. I did not know if he still lived in Ventry, or if it had just been their home back in 1954. I do know, however, that the spirits of Mary and Páid soar together again in the winds over Sceilg Mhichíl.

Perched on the edge of the world (l–r): a beehive hut, high cross and quartz shrine on the top of Sceilg Mhichíl.

Blasket Blessing

'People bare their soul on an island, perhaps that's why romances happen quickly. People are so free.' I pondered Maria's parting words, as I gazed across at the outer islands from the Bright Dwellings. On Sceilg Mhichíl, a very spiritual level of Páid and Mary had been touched. The old man glowed with love for his dead wife and returning to the island to reconnect with her spirit was deeply important to him. I thought of Aisling and Colm, and the other romances that I had seen blossom during that island summer. I thought of Michael, and suddenly I felt very lonely.

The outer islands looked desolate. I flopped onto the heather and stared. An Téaracht stood, a silent sentry, as our most westerly outpost. The lighthouse keepers were long gone. Their little railway, once used to haul supplies up to the lighthouse along precipitous cliffs, was now obsolete. The keepers' nanny goat, which chased Paud O'Connor every time he returned for duty, was dead. Paud, Jo Molloy, Ciaran Ó Broin and men of their calibre were now surplus to requirements, having been made redundant by the great computer.

'And what time of the tide is this to be snorkelling?' had been my first greeting from Paud O'Connor, then the keeper on Hook Lighthouse, County Wexford, several years previously. I had tried bluffing, but it was clear that I hadn't a clue about what I was doing. What followed was a thorough explanation of the tides and currents off Hook Head, along with a firm reprimand. That was delivered over what was to become the first of many warming cups of tea in Hook Lighthouse. A seagull couldn't sneeze without being seen by their 24-hour watch. There is no knowing the number of maritime accidents that lighthouse keepers have prevented over the years. Sadly, their vigilance and human friendship are now just memories, as we bow to the god of automation.

I gazed southwards. There, Sceilig Mhichíl, too, was abandoned. Mick Fitzpatrick was no longer needed to keep watch over his beloved rock. The mighty computer presided behind the barred doors of the lighthouse.

Before me was Inis Mhic Uibhleain. Once again, through my binoculars, I saw the lone figure of Charlie Haughey make his way up to the stones. I wondered what he really thought of Maria's black calf experience. I waved at the now familiar speck in the distance. If it had not been for the lighthouse keepers, he would not have been walking the island that day, or any other day. When his yacht ran aground on rocks at the foot of Mizen Head, it was they who came to his aid in the thick fog. One of them went down a sheer cliff, with only a rope around his waist, to rescue the crew. I'd like to have seen the resident computer trying that stunt. After hundreds of years of invaluable service, the keepers of our Irish lights were very badly let down. I resolved to bring that up with Charlie Haughey the next time we met.

As the rain clouds rolled in from the Atlantic, I left the southern and western seas of Ireland in the hands of two blind, dead lighthouses. It would be sundown soon, time for small drug-smuggling boats to approach our coastline under the noses of our empty automated lighthouses. I vented my frustration as I tramped back along the south path.

On the east of the island, the village was quiet. I stood a while, gazing down at my new home. Maria and the day-trippers had long gone. Sue was busy, in and out of her cottage, hanging freshly dyed yarn on the clothes line. Seán was busy tinkering with the shovel of the yellow digger at the back of the cafe. Sigrid sat at the table outside the hostel, writing. I waved as I strolled down the hill. I felt utterly at home.

As I opened the door of the hut, I stopped to watch the blue ferry returning home, into the island, for the night. It ploughed through the waves, a dusting of seagulls in its wake. Strangely, the binoculars revealed a full complement of passengers. Normally the boat would return empty at this time of the evening.

As the passengers climbed down into the dinghy, it was obvious that they were not coming in to stay on the island. There was not a backpack or a tent between them. Unlike the usual boatload that splintered into different families, nationalities and couples, this entire group gelled with some definite communal purpose. As each dinghy-load climbed above the edge of the cliff, they gathered in a large group, before proceeding slowly up Bóthar na Marbh. Some old ladies linked arms. One thirty-something woman helped an old man up the hill, while a young boy scampered in and out of the crumbling ruins of the deserted village.

At the remains of the old schoolhouse, they stopped. The old building yawned roofless, with gables as jagged as shark's teeth. The lintels and stone sills of the windows remained intact. In front of the doorway, I saw a little table, covered in a white cloth and balanced on two fish boxes. Immediately, I recognised Sue's three prized nasturtium blossoms, fluttering in a glass.

An old frail priest began the ritual of preparing the altar. A younger priest unfolded the vestments. Gently, he placed the garment over the head of the old man, carefully settling the cloth around him. Sigrid and I arrived as the congregation arranged itself on the grassy bank around the old National School. A herring gull landed purposefully on the seaward gable.

As the mass began, the Atlantic clouds banked over the island again. A few drops were the cursory warning before the downpour. A black umbrella held over the white vestments proved futile against horizontal sheets of rain.

Young Father Tom spoke in Irish. It was his second mass *faoin aimsir* and the second time that it had rained. They would not be asking him a third time, he said, smiling. It was also appropriate that this Mass of the Assumption would be held before the schoolhouse since it was here that the women recited the Rosary while the men were out on the mainland at mass. As the priests recited the prayers, an age-old tradition was revived, the rhythm of ritual invoking the lives of the past.

The showers came and went, as they had always done. After Communion, a full rainbow bridged the Blasket Sound. As the final prayers concluded, Micheál de Mordha, Director of the Blasket Heritage Centre, came forward. He explained the islanders' final departure from the island in November 1953. He indicated the remains of the Kearney home, just below the school.

Young Seán Kearney died of suspected meningitis during the appalling Christmas of 1946. Winds raged at over eighty miles per hour for days, with no lull, during which the body

Father Tom saying mass in front of the ruined schoolhouse, watched by a herring gull perched on the seaward gable.

could have been taken to the mainland for a religious burial. There was no church on the island, and no consecrated ground to bury human remains. For more than a week, the corpse of the young man lay on a white sheet in the kitchen.

The distraught family kept an uninterrupted vigil with the body all that time. They were without provisions from the mainland for the wake but, more distressingly, they were without the comfort of a priest. Meanwhile the storms raged relentlessly.

In the second week, one frantic islander went to the schoolhouse and fell to his knees, imploring Our Lady for help. Within the hour, the storm broke, long enough for a *naomhóg* to row out to the mainland for help. It took another two days before the lifeboat from Valentia could reach the island.

That was it, for many of the islanders. The stark reality of not being able to reach a doctor or a priest hit them deeply. A consensus was taken to leave the Great Blasket Island and so, in November 1953, the island was evacuated. Many people obviously wonder why it had taken so long to resettle such a small number of ageing families on the mainland. It has been suggested that Éamon de Valera's government deliberately delayed the relocation to ensure that the problem would emigrate or die off naturally. So the islanders had to wait for seven long years after the death of Seán Kearney, during which time the population of the Great Blasket Island dropped from fifty to twenty-two before the government conceded to the expense of buying four cottages on the mainland in Dún Chaoin.

The story finished, and Micheál sat onto the bank once more. The congregation remained silent, reluctant to break its link with the past. After the final blessing, the herring gull swooped out to sea, and the tie was broken.

As people stirred and began to trickle back down through the ruins, I took the opportunity to approach Father Tom. He agreed to come up to the hut. I raced up ahead of him, lit a candle and an incense stick, and straightened the old chair in under the shelf. There was no other piece of furniture to tidy. Then Father Tom's black-suited legs appeared outside the low doorway. I invited him in, warning him about the low lintel. Once inside, I noted his eyes lingering on the ferns and plants growing from the stone walls. I offered him a seat on my one sheepskin-clad chair. He preferred to stand, his back to the hillside, facing the tiny window, set between the bunk and the chair. As he blessed the dwelling, he sprinkled holy water on the four walls. He prayed in Irish and English, for the owner of the dwelling, Ray Stagles, and his late wife, Joan. He prayed for the past inhabitants, and the future inhabitants. As the candles flickered, and the surf roared below on the White Strand, I said a silent prayer of thanks to the Island Spirit.

Father Tom finished his blessing. Then he slowly replaced the top on the bottle of holy water. Neither of us spoke. The smell of incense and the sound of the sea filled the air. Suddenly I wondered how I could thank him. Before I could offer a cup of tea or of water, he shook my hand. 'Thank you,' he said. 'It's a long time since a priest has been of service to an island house.' I protested that it was I who owed him thanks. He smiled, saying that it was an honour to be welcomed into an island home. He wrote a short note in Irish, for me to pass on to Ray Stagles. Suddenly he noticed through the tiny window that the island was once more deserted, and his flock was aboard the ferry.

Again, he shook my hand. '*Slán agus beannacht.*' He bent low under the lintel and was gone.

A rainbow bridging the Blasket Sound, viewed from outside the hut.

Making Memories

Next morning as I woke to the robin's noisy pecking, I became aware of a faint smell of incense in the air. I did not stir, relishing the scent, the only trace of the previous evening. The smell triggered a stream of fragmented images in my drowsy mind: white vestments under a black umbrella, a herring gull, Seán Kearney's remains on the kitchen table, Maria shouting at a black calf, and Charlie Haughey gazing at the ancient stones. All had become yesterday's memories, as short-lived as seaspray in the wind. With my fingers, I traced the delicate filigree of the fern that grew from the hut wall and overhung my pillow. Soon that too would be a memory, washed away by a new tide. I recalled Charlie Haughey's idea of keeping an island log, and all at once it was vital to record the island mass. I had not mentioned it in the previous night's story. I sat up, startling the robin that ducked out under the eaves. I reached for my journal and pen, returned to the warmth of my bed and began to write about the people and events of the previous day.

By half past eight, I was finished. Four pages of words that would form the sequence of a day's events in the lives of these people, long after the Island Spirit had reclaimed their souls. I lay, listening to the rollers crashing on the White Strand. Their rhythm had become my heartbeat. I wriggled out of my sleeping bag, pulling a shirt around me, and opened my little green door to the sea and the sky. A shiver of excitement ran through me. Over the previous few weeks, everything had begun to change. I was no longer observing my life from outside a window, but I was actually in there, and was sensing each moment. The grass was wet and cold underfoot as I climbed up to the well. I drank and splashed my face with fresh water.

Below, the dolphin played around the buoys, ducking, diving and launching himself into mid-air, with a shudder rippling through his whole body. Seizing the moment, as a memory in the making, I decided to go to the cove, instead of the beach, for my dip. The dolphin ignored me on the beach, and I had never had the nerve to go to the cove until that day.

There was no sign of Seán over at the cafe, or of Sue, below at her house, where her yellow door remained closed. Sigrid had gone out on the previous evening's ferry, to book her return flight to Germany. All was quiet. I ran down the wet path. The ruin of the schoolhouse was empty but for the stonechat, bobbing in and out of his nest in the wall. The mass had melted into the island's past.

The cove was deserted, save for Fergal's inflatable dinghy, pulled up on the slipway, clear of the tide. The water was deep and so very cold. I gasped, treading water furiously, to catch my breath. Several times I had watched the Irish College students stroking the dolphin from the dinghy. One girl had jumped in, and he swam around her as she tried to touch him. I had been fascinated.

Suddenly I was nervous. I had no idea what 13 feet of solid dolphin would look like in the water. Methodically, I began my morning routine of front crawl, backstroke and floating on my back. Below me, a meadow of oarweed drifted in the tide. Just as I decided to get out, there he was. A huge dorsal fin circled me and then it dived. I looked frantically but I could see nothing. I ducked under, just in time to see the shape of a beautiful bottlenose dolphin swim past me. My heart pounded. He had been within a foot of me, but I had not dared to touch him. I waited. Nothing. I duck-dived, kicking hard, down to the oarweed. There was no sign of him. I gripped a couple of tough stems, anchoring myself. Back on the surface, the sun sparkled. Shafts of light filtered down, glinting off the swaying of the seaweed. Then from the hazy distance, a silhouette glided towards me. The dolphin's beak was inches from my face. He turned his head to the left, so his right eye looked straight into mine. For those few seconds, the ache in my lungs disappeared. I reached out, stroking along the side of the dolphin's head. His eye closed and he pushed against my hand. I touched him once more before shooting back up, my lungs bursting.

I gasped at the surface, my whole body tingling. I laughed aloud, as the dolphin circled me, and leaped clear over my head. Each time I duck-dived and swam, he shadowed me, inches from my right side. The more I rubbed and tickled him, the closer he swam.

After a short time, I was exhausted. I trod water, labouring for breath. What strange, helpless creatures they must think we are. Despite his huge weight and size, he was unconditionally protective and gentle, as if I was a baby in the water. Suddenly I felt his beak nuzzle the soles of my feet from below. I couldn't oblige him with a reaction. He then swam to my side and stopped. As I ran my hands down his flanks, he began to move forward, gently, towing me a few feet. I was very cautious, afraid that he would feel trapped, but each time I let him go, he returned, offering another piggyback. I avoided his blowhole carefully, stroking from head to tail, as I was towed in circles around the cove. I began to wonder if it was my laughter that kept bringing him back. I felt sheer delight pulsing in every cell of my body. Maybe my voice was familiar to him at that stage. For over six weeks, I had called to him from the beach every morning.

As I swam towards the slipway, the dolphin kept swimming between the shore and me, but there wasn't an ounce of energy left in my body to play any more. I felt a rock under the water, and found my balance. I could stand with my head and shoulders out of the water. The dolphin glided over to me, stopping, with his beak tipping my chin. He never moved while I chatted and scratched his throat. Each time I rubbed him, he allowed me to lift his beak farther and farther up out of the water, until his head rested on my shoulder. Once again his eye held my gaze.

As his head slid gently back down my arm into the water, he opened his beak wide, making chatty clicking sounds. I stroked the side of his head and the inside of his beak before he closed his mouth gently on my hand, as softly as velvet.

Finally, as I scrambled out onto the slipway, he circled the cove. My feet had absolutely no feeling and I couldn't stand. Hugging my knees in an effort to get warm, I pulled my shirt around me. All the while, I continued to talk to him through chattering teeth. Only as I disappeared over the clifftop did he swim out to sea.

Back at the hut, I made a hot pot of rice porridge and drank huge amounts of tea to warm up. I sat on a stone, leaning back against the warm wall, looking across to the mainland, cradling the warm saucepan in my freezing hands. Blue sky and blue sea mirrored one another in all directions. The Three Sisters stretched out into the sea, side by side, leaning on their green elbows, their toes interlaced somewhere back at Brandon

Creek. A cow bawled from Firtear's farm on Slea Head. Cars glinted in the sunshine on the clifftop above Dún Chaoin pier, but there was still no sign of the ferry. The mainland was a world away.

Half a metre from my elbow, a young rabbit nibbled the grass. The donkeys ambled up the path. The mare was so heavily in foal, her belly was inches above the grass. They stopped below me. 'No joy today, sorry.' I called. 'The cupboard is bare – no apples, no carrots, no donkey food, no rabbit food, no robin food.' The stallion was having none of it and seized his opportunity to stage a coup. He had cantered up the bank into the hut before I could struggle on to my numb feet. There was barely room for the two of us in there. As he chewed up a page of my journal, I attempted to push him backwards through the door. Turning him around was not an option, unless he was going to clamber over the bunk. In the middle of the struggle, Sue arrived and lent a hand, pulling him back by the tail.

She shooed the two donkeys down past *Teach an Rí*, while I made some more tea. 'No ferry today,' she announced. 'Fergal is in Dingle with engine trouble.' She was delighted with the break. Things had been hectic lately. 'I'll get to relax and do a few jobs around the house, catch up on some weaving, and you know what? I might even go to the beach for an hour this afternoon.'

I handed her a mug of tea, and we settled back against the warm wall once more. It had started and was continuing to be a wonderful day on the island. 'That's great,' I said. 'I won't go to the back of the island. It'll be bliss to stay around the village in the sunshine and read.' We sat quietly, watching the chough family flying along the cliff line below Páidí's house. Already the chicks seemed to be as big and as fast as their parents. Down on the White Strand, the Beverley Sisters were hauling out into the sunshine, at the far end of the beach. 'They must have heard the news too.'

The whole island seemed set for a peaceful day.

'So tell me about Donie.' I had no idea that Sue had seen me swimming with the dolphin that morning. Just as I began to tell her, it started. It began with the deep, gravelly scraping. Then there was the creaky swivelling, followed by the heavy thud. The whole pattern of noise was underpinned by an incessant whining. Sue looked in disbelief at me, saying nothing for a while. Then she held her hands over her ears. 'I don't believe it. He's obviously got word that there's no visitors coming in. He'll be at that all day. I can't stick it.'

I knew what she meant. Each evening, as the last tourist ferry left the tranquillity of the Great Blasket Island, the yellow digger emerged from behind the cafe. Since it was a tourist-free day, Sue was probably right. We were in for it! For some reason the noise resounded through the stone village, and was twice as loud at her house.

'That's the end of my weaving for the day. I'll go out of my mind listening to that.'

'What is he doing anyway?'

I had seen quite a difference since my first school visit to the island. Peig Sayers's house had become a 22-bed hostel. Next door to that, the Buffer Keane's house had become the cafe, while his old cowshed boasted flush toilets and a rather ripe septic tank. I dreaded further development of the island, yet it seemed inevitable. Since I had arrived, the piles of concrete blocks, white aeroboard insulation and areas cordoned off by yards of yellow fluorescent tape had increased dramatically. Sue still sat with her hands firmly over her ears.

The ownership battle had been waged for as long as she could remember. Did the Great Blasket Island belong to the nation, the Office of Public Works, the wealthy American, the islanders' descendants or the local entrepreneur? In poorer economic times, some islanders' descendants had sold their holdings to the wealthy American who had, in turn, sold the few holdings to a local buyer. The government had failed to make the island a National Monument as the hand of justice ruled in favour of the purchaser, and so the Great Blasket Island entered the era of Ireland's construction boom. In recent weeks, things had been happening quickly, as the powerboat zoomed in and out to the beach, loaded with building materials.

As Sue described what she knew of the planned development, I could feel my heart sink. All would be advertised as adding to the authenticity of that Great Blasket Experience, no doubt. The scraping, whining and dumping continued as a rising tide of frustration surged through me. I saw myself mounting my high horse and so I promptly bit my lip. I could see Sue was in a tough position. Living, as she was, in such close proximity to people on the island, and depending on each other, it was difficult to criticise. It was fine for me to breeze in and expostulate.

I hobbled up to the *Dáil* with my mug of tea, glancing towards the cafe as nonchalantly as possible. The digger was scraping away the soil, old walls and ditches at the back of the Buffer Keane's house. I came back to report on the proceedings, but on seeing Sue visibly upset, I changed the subject. I tried to distract her with an animated account of Donie's earlier antics in the water. My forced jollity served only to make us both more conscious of the persistent noise. 'There's no escaping it, is there?' I conceded.

We sat for a while longer the sunshine. Only then were my feet finally beginning to warm up after nearly two hours in the water. 'More tea?'

'I think that tea bag died a few days ago, don't you?'

I had to admit she was right.

'I think I'll stick with my original plan,' she mused, eyes closed as she leaned back against the wall. 'I'll just move farther out, find another island when they develop this one.'

Her fatalism disturbed me. Yet, maybe she was right; maybe it was inevitable. The spores of the Celtic Tiger were sprouting a blight of holiday homes and so-called authentic Irish PVC cottage complexes all over Ireland's coastline. Perhaps it was only a matter of time before it spread to the islands. 'Right. It's pointless sitting here helplessly, not knowing what's going on.' I got to my feet, gathering up the mugs and saucepan.

'What are you going to do?' Sue asked, squinting up into the sunshine.

'I'm going to ask him out straight what he's doing.'

'He's not going to tell you. To be fair, I'm sure he's only told each day what work he's to do.'

'Well, if I don't ask, I won't know that.'

Sue slid down onto the path. 'Good luck. I'm going to try to weave for the day. Call down and let me know if you wangle anything out of him.'

Inside the hut, the noise of the digger engine reverberated. I packed my backpack for a day at the back of the island. There could be no pleasure on the east side of the island with that constant droning. I had no food left to take with me, so I had the perfect excuse to interrupt Seán. I would buy some food and strike up a conversation.

The Ghost at the Buffer Keane's

I set off towards Peig's house. The scraping, swivelling and dumping got louder as I approached. The padlocks were closed on the half-doors. Bobbles of aeroboard swirled on the ground between Peig's and the Buffer Keane's. The yellow digger was in action behind the Buffer's house. 'Hello,' I roared at the top of my voice. The scraping of metal on stone was deafening. The cab rotated mechanically from side to side between the stone walls and the dump truck. All the while, Seán's back was facing me. I lifted the fluorescent yellow tape and ducked underneath. The back of the cafe was littered with yellow gas bottles, abandoned batteries and fish boxes full of glass bottles. I winced on the sharply broken rock underfoot. 'Hello,' I called again, with a little less conviction. I was not quite sure how he was going to react to halting his work for the sale of a jam scone.

He looked at me curiously for a few seconds before he turned off the engine. Silence. I could imagine Sue's relief at the other side of the village. Since he did not move, I hobbled over painfully. 'Hello,' I called again, managing the biggest smile I could muster. 'I was wondering if I could buy a few things in the cafe?' That sounded better than saying one scone, which I could obviously have got from Sue. 'Sorry for interrupting. My supplies are getting a bit low.' He still did not move.

I began to feel quite a fraud. For all the times that I had been over to the hostel to visit Laura and Sigrid, and into the cafe to buy Aisling her lunch, I had never really spoken to Seán. Suddenly, there I was, beaming at him as if we were great friends. Eventually, he climbed off the digger and approached me.

'Sorry for disturbing you. I was wondering if I could buy a few things in the cafe. I'm running a bit low.' The hypocrisy of it! Swearing not to encourage commercial development on the island while I proceeded to buy scones and chocolate from him. Sue had pointed out, however, that a fact-finding operation could be classified as mitigating circumstances, so I didn't feel quite so bad about purchasing the items. I followed him around and into the cafe.

'You're staying over in Ray's house.'

'Yes.'

'It's fairly basic, as far as I remember.'

'I suppose it is really, but it has everything I need. It's great to have the use of it.'

'Haven't seen you around much.'

'No, I usually go walking every day.' Suddenly, his little puppy, Captain Jack, appeared from behind the counter and took an instant shine to my bare ankles. Having dodged around the tables several times, I ended up squatting on one of the chairs, laughing with the enemy. It turned out that, like me, Seán was from County Kilkenny. He had worked only a few miles from my parents' home, before taking the job on the Great Blasket Island. Gradually, he appeared to be less and less of the commercial ogre I had previously imagined him to be. He loved working on the island, especially in the winter before the tourist season, when it was quiet. I sat in amazement. Sue had a lot more in common with Seán than she realised. Somehow, I could not reconcile this gentle, island-loving and puppy-loving man with the development around me.

'Do you take sugar?' he asked.

'No, thank you.' He handed me a mug of tea, as I continued to crouch on the chair in an attempt to keep my toes out of Captain Jack's mouth. Seán drank his tea gazing down at the surf breaking on the White Strand.

I directed all my attention to patting Captain Jack's head. What was I doing here? To mention the digger, the building plans or anything else, seemed inappropriate now. I adored the strong tea. It was a far cry from the coloured water I had shared with Sue earlier. 'The old wooden counter is very nice. I haven't been inside here before.'

'That's the pub counter that was used in the filming of *Ryan's Daughter*.'

'Really!' I was captivated. Operation Fact-Finder was on permanent hold.

I began to describe the film scene as it played out in my memory. 'The village idiot, played by John Mills, sat on a stool at the bar counter. He grinned inanely at Christopher Jones, a shell-shocked First World War officer, who sat drinking, drowning his sorrows at a bar table, about there. The idiot kept kicking the counter. Bang, bang, bang. It got louder and louder. The camera zoomed in on his boot, kicking and kicking. The sweat broke out on the lieutenant's face, until the banging exploded into gunfire in his mind, and he collapsed to the floor, a helpless wreck convulsed in spasm. John Mills was brilliant. I'll never forget that boot kicking the counter. I'm surprised there isn't a dent in it from all the kicking.' I went over and checked along the bottom of the counter – not a mark.

'How many times did you see the film?' Seán was looking at me in astonishment.

'Twice. I was quite young the first time, and it was then that the kicking really impressed me. I think it was because it shocked me so much. It was frightening, I suppose.' The second time, the scenery, the storm on Coumenoule Beach and the views of the Blasket Islands impressed me most.'

I was economical with the truth, omitting to say that it was the love scene in the bluebells that held the greatest appeal for me as a teenager. During my boarding-school days, every second Saturday, we were shown a *suitable* film with the projector in the study hall. Any time that there was a threat of romance, Sister Ursula's censoring hand was clamped over the projector, blacking out the screen, to the groans of a hundred pubescent girls. On the night we saw *Ryan's Daughter*, she was called outside the door for a message, at the most opportune of moments. The bluebells left a thrilling impression on my teenage imagination.

I finished my tea and replaced my mug reverently onto the *Ryan's Daughter* counter. 'I better let you get back to work. Thanks for the tea, Seán.'

'No bother. I was stopping for a break anyway. I'll keep at it till it gets dark. Need to catch up, while the ferries are off. Call in again.'

'Thanks. Bye.' I set off, along the north path, up at the back of the Buffer Keane's, and the yellow digger roared into action again. As I rounded the turn and met the westerly breeze and the soaring kittiwakes, the digger ceased to exist. I spent until mid-afternoon wandering the cliffs and watching the birds at the back of the island.

On my return I hesitated at the crossroads. Taking the south road would mean passing Sue's house without a wisp of information. Taking the north road would mean passing above the cafe and hostel again, getting a bird's eye view of the work in progress. I took the north road, changing the bag to my left shoulder to protect it from the sun beating down from above An Téaracht. *An Fear Marbh* lay basking in the heat, hands clasped serenely over his great stomach. We had made our peace. I watched the changing shadows over his huge bulk until I rounded the path towards the village, leaving him behind. I braced myself for the noise of the digger. There was none. The closer I got, the clearer it became that the digger and dump truck had not moved from where Seán had left them that morning. As I passed, he suddenly appeared from the side of the hostel and waved at me. I waved back and began to zigzag down the hill.

'Good walk?'

'Lovely, thanks. There's going to be another amazing sunset tonight.'

'I heard the lunchtime forecast. We're in for another scorcher tomorrow too.'

I glanced over towards the digger. 'Are you on strike?' I smiled. I knew he hesitated. I could see him looking for an answer.

'Ah, the ground is too slippery under the digger.' I looked at the earth. It appeared to be bone dry to me, but I said nothing. I adjusted my bag. I could feel that I had definitely got too much sun.

'Will you have a cup of tea? I was just making one.' I accepted gratefully. 'So, when are you off back to work?' he asked.

I could feel my stomach lurch. I had succeeded in quashing the thought of leaving up until then. I greeted and made a fuss of Captain Jack in an attempt to avoid the question.

We sat at a table looking out over the White Strand. He produced a pot of tea and a lemon cake, much to my delight.

After sitting in silence for a while Seán said, 'I hear you saw something over near Ray's.' He continued to look out the window. I knew I was not going to be ridiculed so I told him about my encounter with the two little girls.

'Did you ever see anything else?' he asked, as if I was leaving something out.

'No. Nothing else and that was a few weeks ago now.'

He did not say anything as he continued to stare out the window.

'Why? What have you seen?' I asked. I felt sure there was something. He shrugged and took another drink of tea.

'I don't believe in things like that.'

'I know. Nobody does, but what did you see?'

'It started maybe three months ago, when I started working out the back. I didn't mind it at first. I ignored it, but it kept getting stronger. I was in on the island working by myself then. There was nobody else here. The weather was dire. Even Sue had gone out to the mainland. There was *nobody* else on the island.'

'What got stronger? What was it?'

'I used to feel that I was being watched. I didn't mind it first, but it became so intense. You couldn't ignore it, like there was someone breathing over your shoulder. It got really bad over a three-day period. On the third day, the feeling came over me as soon as I went out. That was the first time I was really nervous. When I looked around, there was a dark shadow of a figure standing behind the cafe. It was tall and wore a high hat. I couldn't make out the features, but I knew it was watching me. Then, it gradually faded as I was looking at it. I know I saw it. I stopped working out the back for the rest of that day.

'Next day, the boss came in and the ferry was running too, so he told me to put the digger away. The minute I turned the key in the ignition, I got the feeling again but I deliberately didn't look at the thing. It makes you really uneasy though. Then I was told to take the inflatable dinghy round to the Gravel Beach, to check out something. I had that awful sensation the whole time. It was so strong that I couldn't bear to look back up to the island.

'I had never capsized until that day. The wave just came out of nowhere. Luckily, the ferry was in, and the lads came over to pull me out, but I felt a bit shook after it. The boss told me to take the rest of the day off, so I came back up here to dry off. At the top of the stairs over there, I got a powerful heavy feeling again. The shadow was there once more, but now it was actually inside the house. I was probably weak and frozen from being in the water so long, but I lost my footing and fell down the stairs. First time that ever happened to me and I stone sober. Some of the girls that worked in the cafe over the years said that there was something strange in this house. They didn't like sleeping upstairs here at all.'

I felt quite uneasy, as I looked over his shoulder at the wooden stairs at the far side of the *Ryan's Daughter* counter.

'I'm always so careful about locking in Captain Jack when I'm working. I keep the bottom half of the door closed and I always check it. I don't know how he got out. This happened on the morning after I'd capsized. I went out to start work and somehow the pup followed me out. The minute I turned the ignition, I got the suffocating feeling again. I could hardly breathe. As I felt it, the shadow of the man crossed right on front of the dump truck. I won't repeat what I said to it, but I just drove forward, ignoring it.' He stopped talking for a minute as he fondled Captain Jack's ears. The pup had his front paws on Seán's lap with his nose cradled between his knees. His two big brown eyes looked up mischievously. 'Anyway, the wheel rolled forward, right on top of this little fella.' I could feel his guilt and upset still as he said it. 'That meant back across into Dingle for a few weeks of visits to the vet. You'd never guess to look at him now, would you?'

As I reached down to pat Captain Jack, he scampered over to lick my hand and tug at the tail of my shirt again. I picked him up onto my lap and ran my hands down the length of his body. 'Not a bit. He looks perfect.'

'Well, the few weeks in Dingle held the work up again. There's a lot to do in the cafe and hostel, so it was mad busy when I got back into the island.' I could appreciate that, but somehow I couldn't help feeling that he was reluctant to start up the digger again.

'So how was it being back in?' I urged him on.

'Fine. Nothing . . . just like it had been before.' He hesitated again.

'You didn't feel anything?'

'No. While I was busy in the hostel and the kitchen – nothing.'

'So why did you stop work at the back today? The ground wasn't slippery.'

'A while before you interrupted me, I felt it again. That was why I was a bit slow to turn around. I was a bit taken aback when I saw that it was only you.'

'I thought you were annoyed at being interrupted.'

'Not at all. When you're weeks in here alone, it's great to meet someone and have a chat, not to mention someone from Kilkenny!' he smiled.

'So what did you do when you felt it today?'

'Just ignored it. I'm behind on the foundations. I have to get ahead with the work. I just told the thing where to go and I'll beat it. That's the answer.' That seemed to be an end to it, as far as Seán was concerned. I was not so sure. I felt genuinely worried for him.

'Have you told your boss about it? Maybe you should tell him to stop the excavations.'

His look said it all. He didn't speak for some time and then: 'Maybe it was a trick of the light. Maybe when you're on your own for a while you begin to see things.'

I thought about this for a while. 'Perhaps you do begin to see things. However, it doesn't mean that they're not there. Maybe when you're on your own for a while you become quiet enough on the inside to be sensitive to other wavelengths. Like the dial on an old wireless, the slower and more sensitively you turn it, the more stations you pick up. Flicking madly from one thing to another, as we do in today's world, we miss most of what is around us. I don't think you imagined that man. I don't think that I imagined the two young girls, but I do think that you have to be in a certain frame of mind to be aware of them. I know that I wouldn't see the two girls now.'

I didn't know if that made any sense to him, but it was beginning to, for me.

'So, what's going on? What is this fella with the hat doing behind the cafe, and what's he got to do with me?'

'I don't know. The patch of ground that you're excavating – what was it originally?'

'It's only the back haggard, outbuildings and walls of the old house here. Used to belong to a man called the Buffer Keane.'

'Well, maybe it's him and he doesn't want you digging up the back garden, walls and sheds he spent a lifetime building.' I could feel the frustration of my earlier conversation with Sue resurfacing. 'I know they only look like a few old stones to us, but there are layers of real people's lives in that ground. Maybe they want it left alone.'

'If that is the case, nothing new would ever be built. The

showers and toilets are needed. You can't expect people to live as they did a hundred years ago. It will all be tastefully done. There'll be a fifty-seat restaurant and the cottages will be restored to show tourists what the original dwellings looked like.'

I could feel my colour rising, but I bit my lip. What was the point in venting my frustration on Seán? He was only doing his job.

'I think the Interpretative Centre on the mainland does that job already. That's where the restaurants, exhibitions, reconstructions, interactive displays and bookshop are. That's where they belong. It's a window into the layers of Blasket history and life. Then people come over here to experience that beauty, isolation and spirit. After what's happened to you, do you not think the island should be left to its spirits and to nature?'

'I can't see what harm a few buildings will do.' We sat in silence for a while. Neither of us wanted to argue.

I thought of Inis Mhic Uibhleain where Charlie Haughey had said he felt like shaking the stones. 'They know all the secrets of the past,' he had said. He had left them intact, however. I kept my thoughts to myself.

'I don't want to see the island overdeveloped either, but facilities are needed,' Seán continued.

We had come to a stalemate. I poured him another cup of tea as a peace offering.

'Well, I don't think the Buffer Keane will let go of his back haggard that easily. Sugar?'

Just then Seán's mobile rang. I jumped out of my skin. It was a sound that had become very unfamiliar. He picked it up. 'It's the boss,' he said, moving over to the doorway where the signal was stronger. I played with Captain Jack. The call was short. Seán came back and sat down, flattening his hair back on his head. He said nothing. I sat looking as disinterested as I possibly could. I was not going to say anything, but I did not have to.

'Planning permission has been delayed. I have to stop work out the back again.' He looked stunned.

'You're joking!'

'No, he's just got word.'

I raised my mug in the direction of the staircase. 'To the spirit of the Buffer Keane and his back garden.'

Once I passed the *Dáil* and was out of view of the cafe, I dumped my bag and raced down the path to Sue's. I was laughing and shaking with excitement. The island was safe. Well, for another while anyway.

The Ebbing Tide

The evenings were drawing in by the end of August. The crisp scent of autumn carried over the waves to the island. Fewer day-trippers visited the Great Blasket Island, as families backed up and returned home for another winter of work, school-runs, football matches, and homework. Aisling closed up the bookshop in *Teach an Rí* and returned to Galway for her next year of secondary school. Sigrid walked the island one last time and returned to Germany for another year of teaching kindergarten. One morning, the dolphin disappeared out to sea and we did not see him again. The sheep men collected the last of the fleeces from the *clochán* down at Páidí Dunleavy's. We chatted and laughed, but I had no tea left to offer. They warned me they'd be looking for cake, too, the following summer. I watched their boat fade from view on the ebbing tide into the mist under Dún Mór Head. As each ferry left the island for the mainland, my stomach tightened in its wake.

Then, one morning, it was my turn to leave. Once the robin had woken me at daybreak, I was alert and ready to savour every precious last moment. As I lay listening to the thundering of the waves, I wondered how I would ever sleep without their soothing rhythm. Outside, every sound and scent was heightened. As I wove my way down through the maze of tumbling walls and gables to the clifftop, I was saturated with sensation. The chill wet dew on the grass sent shivers of anticipation through me. Blue sea, green headlands, orange lichen and yellow tormentil flashed around me, more boldly than in any other morning scene. The booming of surf in the shadow of the caves resonated in the pit of my stomach. The rosy red flight of a stonechat would stitch a path through the depths of my mind long after he had disappeared from view.

As I lay back in the water, looking up at the Great Blasket Island, the door of the Buffer Keane's yawned open. To its left, Seán emerged from the white washroom and stood gazing over the Blasket Sound before disappearing into the darkness to prepare for a day of visitors. The two donkeys grazed in a field to the north of the cafe, following their usual pattern. At the other side of the tumble of ruins, Sue's yellow door was open. She appeared suddenly, sluiced a basin of water over the stone wall. Then she returned inside, just as quickly. High in the blue above the slopes behind the village, the chough family called to each other on the wing. The chicks were ready to move on.

I walked my green mile back up to the hut. I felt like one condemned, clinging to the last images of life. In fact, my life was beginning again, restored by the spirit of the island. The prospect of leaving its sanctuary was terrifying. The essential living on the island seemed to bear no resemblance to my previous manic survival on the mainland. I wondered if I could maintain that real life and avoid donning the familiar cloak of illusion.

As I swept out the hut and set fresh candles in all the holders, I felt lost. My bags were piled outside the doorway. I stuffed my sleeping bag and pillow into a plastic bag to keep them dry on the ferry crossing. For the first time in weeks, thoughts of driving the car, checking the answering machine, getting money, paying bills and preparing for work entered my mind and filled me with anxiety. I took my camping stove out of the hut and set it down on the grass. I zipped the car keys safely in the side pocket of my backpack and tied my boots to the strap.

Across the Blasket Sound, cars glinted on the cliff in the sunshine. I wondered if my old Honda was still there. I had not given it a thought all summer. I went back in one last time, before padlocking the green door. The scent of sandalwood still hung in the air. I sat on the bed and touched the lace ferns that grew from the stone wall. Suddenly, the sound of the surf washed through me. The room was filled with the breaking of waves. For some time, I was aware of nothing else. Then I left the hut and locked the door behind me.

With my routine gone, I seemed to be fumbling in slow motion. What should I do next? I walked over to the cafe to say goodbye. Laura was gone out for a walk, so I wrote her a note. I was relieved. It was less painful. Seán was busy preparing food.

'We'll hook up in Kilkenny sometime,' he promised. I knew we wouldn't. He said that he wasn't going to spend another winter in on the island. I felt very awkward, and we shook hands.

I began hauling my stuff down to the ferry. The third fish box of gear was my last load. I nudged it over the bank and it took off like a drunken sledge, dragging me on the end of the rope down the steep path. Finally, after unloading the gear on to the slipway, I was set to climb back up to Sue's with her fish box in tow.

'Customs inspection in ten minutes,' Fergal shouted from the clifftop.

'You'll be disappointed,' I called back. The rule was: anything that could be consumed or burned stayed in on the island. My box of candles, new batteries, matches and remaining morsels of food were all with Sue and Laura. I took one last look back at my baggage. I spotted the sheep fleece that had covered my bed at night and my chair during the day. Sue would have more use for it than I would. I rolled it up and put it into the fish box.

'You're a different person to the one who arrived here at the start of the summer,' Sue said as we hugged. I don't remember if I answered. I just thought how true it was. Like a shattered vase, somehow my fragmented spirit had been reconstructed.

I climbed up the path to the old National School and stopped at the place where I had seen the two little girls. I pressed my bare toes into the softness of the grass and breathed in the warmth of the island. It had touched and healed a wound that the living could not see.

I was the only passenger on *Oileán na nÓg*. I leaned against the rail, looking back up at the island that filled the sky. The boat rocked gently. All was quiet, but for the slapping of the sea against the hull. After a while, Fergal emerged from the wheelhouse. 'It's going to be another hot one. Last day?'

I nodded, unsure of my voice. He did not seem to notice.

'We're in no rush.' He opened the fiddle case. 'The sea air is terrible on stringed instruments.' He began tuning the strings. 'Even an hour in this atmosphere and the strings are affected.' Without another word, he leaned back against the rail and the music of the fiddle resonated in the caves, rising up the cliffs and over the Great Blasket Island. The notes sparkled on the surface of the water and I did not hide my tears any longer.

As we set off, Sue waved from the low wall outside her house. I waved back and watched her disappear inside the door. The figure of Seán stood outside the half-door of the cafe, a little white dot scampering around his feet, before they too disappeared. Soon, their houses merged into the jumble of ruins, and the ruins, in turn, gradually merged into the silhouette of the island. I sat on the ferry and watched the Great Blasket Island recede between the blue arch of the sky and the white fantail of the ferry's wash. Waves of loneliness flooded through me, as they had for generations of island farewells before me, and as they would for generations to come.

The Great Blasket Island.

Glossary

alanna	anglicised version of 'a leanbh', meaning 'my child'
asthore	anglicised version of 'a stór', meaning 'my treasure', 'my dear'
bothán	small shed or cabin
clochán	stone beehive hut
colleen	anglicised version of 'cailín', meaning 'girl'
currach	small wooden-framed boat covered in waterproof material
dáil	assembly house for meetings and distributing the post
Dia dhaoibh	greeting when meeting more than one person, literally 'God be with you (pl)'
Dia dhuit	greeting when meeting one person, literally 'God be with you'
fáilte isteach	'welcome inside'
faoin aimsir	outside, exposed to the weather
Fear Marbh	literally 'the dead man', popular name for Inis Tuaisceart. Also known as the Sleeping Giant
naomhóg	a currach or coracle
Oileán na nÓg	the island of the young
púcaí	spirits, fairies
seisiún	traditional Irish music session
slán	'goodbye'
slán agus beannacht	'goodbye and God bless'
Teach an Rí	the King's house